The Meaning of Michelle

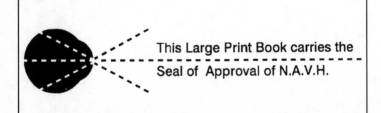

This Large Print Book carries the
Seal of Approval of N.A.V.H.

THE MEANING
OF MICHELLE

16 WRITERS ON THE ICONIC FIRST LADY AND HOW HER JOURNEY INSPIRES OUR OWN

EDITED BY
VERONICA CHAMBERS

THORNDIKE PRESS
A part of Gale, Cengage Learning

GALE
CENGAGE Learning®

Farmington Hills, Mich • San Francisco • New York • Waterville, Maine
Meriden, Conn • Mason, Ohio • Chicago

GALE
CENGAGE Learning®

**LIBRARY OF CONGRESS CIP DATA ON FILE.
CATALOGUING IN PUBLICATION FOR THIS BOOK
IS AVAILABLE FROM THE LIBRARY OF CONGRESS**

ISBN-13: 978-1-4104-9886-1 (hardcover)
ISBN-10: 1-4104-9886-7 (hardcover)

Published in 2017 by arrangement with St. Martin's Press, LLC

Printed in Mexico
1 2 3 4 5 6 7 21 20 19 18 17

For Jason

CONTENTS

8

PREFACE

AVA DUVERNAY

Allow me to set the scene with one comprehensive, yet glorious run-on sentence . . . A junior African-American senator captures the Democratic nomination against the former president's wife then goes on to handily defeat a war hero to become the leader of the free world with his stunning wife, who happens to be a graduate of Princeton and Harvard Law, by his side.

Yep. The story would be astonishing in its audacity and seeming implausibility if it weren't true. As Winston Churchill once said, "The truth is incontrovertible. Malice may attack it. Ignorance may deride it. But in the end; there it is."

Despite the Clintons, McCain, Palin, Wright, Ayers, despite all the malice and the ignorance, the truth is incontrovertible indeed. Barack and Michelle Obama served this country for two terms as President and First Lady of the United States of America.

Imagine that. America shaped in the image of a black man — with a black woman by his side. Even after eight years of watching them daily in the press, the fact that the most powerful man in the world is a Black man is still breathtaking to me. The fact that he goes home to a tight-knit, loving family headed by a Black woman is soul-stirring. That woman is Michelle. Michelle! That name now carries a whole world of meaning. And a whole world of memory. And a whole world of magic.

In an interview with *The New York Times* in 2009, President Obama shared this gem to encourage further insight: "What I value most about my marriage is that it is separate and apart from a lot of the silliness of Washington, and Michelle is not a part of that silliness." Indeed, First Lady Michelle Obama is anything but silly. She's never been that.

I remember watching her on November 10, 2008. On that fall afternoon, the most famous dress to grace the White House was not Monica Lewinsky's blue travesty, but the deep red shift worn by Michelle as she toured her new home. Damn being demure! The sight of her striding up the White House steps was a transformative image to behold. The first White House visit was historic, but the boldness of the future First Lady said it all. In one wardrobe choice, this stellar sister brought a breath of fresh air to the hallowed halls of the world's most famous residence — and to the rusty old game of politics. In one visit, Michelle supplanted the cartoons of Monica, Katrina and their representative presidencies, ripe with mishandled trust and low morals. In that one photo op, Michelle infused the image of the First Lady with pride, panache and polish. Many of us saw a woman to be admired. A woman to be trusted.

Scratch that.

Many of us saw a Black woman to be admired. A Black woman to be trusted. There it is.

INTRODUCTION: HOMEGIRLS

VERONICA CHAMBERS

Barack Obama's historic run for presidency coincided directly with me becoming a mother. I came back to the United States after a year in France with my husband and two things happened: I had a baby and Obama cinched the nomination. My earliest recollections of motherhood seem to have as a constant backdrop the Obamas on TV, on NPR, in the newspapers and magazines I read. Their name quickly became a sort of lullaby that we used to put the baby to sleep: Oh, Oh, Obama. Oh, Oh, Obama. When I voted for him that November, my daughter was in a sling across my chest. I remember stepping into the voting booth with her and just taking a moment of feeling her breathe against me and thinking of Obama's iconic line, while we breathe we hope, as I pulled the lever and cast my vote.

By the inauguration, I was in full pash mode with Michelle Obama; so much so

15

that I covered my office wall with designer sketches of her inauguration dress. I began my day with *New York* magazine's "The Michelle Obama Look Book." I have loved clothes my whole life, but Michelle Obama took my style obsession to a new level. Black women have shaped and supported the American fashion industry from the earliest days. In 1860, Elizabeth Keckley, a former slave, moved to Washington and set up business as a seamstress. Among her many esteemed clients were Mary Todd Lincoln. From the Harlem Renaissance to the 1960s, 1970s and beyond, black women were both muses and creators of fashion. I was like so many Black women who had grown up loving style icons from Dorothy Dandridge to Diana Ross, to the one-name icons that ranged from Iman to Solange. But we'd never had anyone like Michelle before. She wasn't a model, an actress or a musician. She was, quite simply, the star of her own life — and that was a game changer for Black women, and it turned out all women, in the early twenty-first century.

I was as obsessed as everyone else with her arms. When I began to get up before 5 a.m. to work out with a trainer two days a week before getting to work, I thought of Michelle Obama in Chicago. At the time, we lived in a suburb of New York and getting to the trainer involved leaving my home at 5 a.m. to take two trains into the city. But I was inspired by what Cornell McClellan, her Chicago trainer, told *Women's Health* magazine: "She's truly committed herself to the importance of health and fitness. I believe the purpose of training is to tighten up the slack, toughen the body, and polish the spirit. To do that, we take a holistic approach that includes strength, cardiovascular, and flexibility training." At the end of the day, I think that's what was behind all the shine that her biceps received in the media, both in the United States and all around the world: here was a busy woman who had found the time to take care of herself. She was not last on her to-do list, after her amazing kids and her extraordinary husband. She put herself first — and had done so for a long time.

Around the same time, my daughter, then a toddler, had transformed her nursery lullaby of "Oh, Oh, Obama" into a full-scale Elektra crush on the President of the United States. "Me no like 'Chelle," she would say, glowering at the TV. I was horrified. I wasn't really worried that I was raising a future home wrecker (though the thought did cross my mind). But more, I felt like somehow

I'd failed to convey to my daughter that she and her cohort had been lucky enough to be born with the most amazing role model in the White House, the kind of role model that was unlike any enjoyed by previous generations of brown-skinned girls. "We love 'Chelle," I quickly course-corrected as I brought home every one of the commemorative photo books that were published in those early years of the administration. " 'Chelle is awesome. 'Chelle is the best." Eventually, my daughter got the memo and "Me no like 'Chelle" turned into "I want a play date with 'Chelle and her daughters." To which I replied, "We all do, honey. We all do."

More than one essayist in this anthology refers to the First Lady as 'Chelle. There's an intimacy we felt with her from the beginning. The mainstream media seemed flummoxed by her lack of political posturing: Is she on board with this whole political spouse thing? Do the Obamas want it (meaning the presidency) badly enough? But it was that very same lack of fake warmth and glossed-over royal waves that let us, in the Black community, know that she was real, and this is what won our affection. She wasn't going to bare her soul because, as we used to say on the block, "I don't know you like that." She wasn't going to figure out how and to what extent she'd let us in until the deal was done and we agreed, through the formal process of voting, that they would be our First Family.

Michelle Obama quickly set about making the White House America's home, and it was, of course, during the First Lady's history-setting poetry jam that Lin-Manuel Miranda first debuted what would become the iconic musical *Hamilton.* One of the songs from that musical describes how after the revolution, "the world turned upside down." The election of Barack Obama as the forty-fourth president was not as tumultuous as the American Revolution, but it did coincide with the world turning upside down — in ways both great and horrible — for Black Americans. So we can't look at Michelle Obama and all she has come to represent without considering the corresponding rise of Black women in other fields. The Obamas did not come into office under the auspices of an imagined bluescreen Camelot. Rather, while they moved into the White House, America basked in the genius of Shondaland, the world according to Shonda Rhimes, where we learned the importance of finding your person and getting good with the dark and twisty parts of ourselves. Then Kerry Washington joined the Shonda party and we all got Poped, basking in the power of an onscreen fixer, based on Judy Smith, a real-life Washington, D.C., fixer, a woman who confidently and stylishly stepped into her power. I believe that someday, the GIF of Olivia Pope intoning, "It's handled," will be installed in the National Women's History Museum in Washington, D.C. Once that museum is built, that is.

And yet, for all that Black women have achieved over the last eight years, there have been devastating, unspeakable and senseless acts of violence against members of our community — the kind of killings that brought to mind the 1930s and the days of unchecked lynching. As the singer and fashion muse Solange wrote after the Charleston Church shooting, "Was already weary. Was already heavy hearted. Was already tired. Where can we be safe? Where can we be free? Where can we be black?"

The Black Lives Matter movement, started by three young women, is as powerful a testimony to the advancements of Black women as any move to the corner office or Capitol Hill. Michelle Obama did not flinch from the more socially heartbreaking moments of the Obamas' eight years in the White House. Witness her defiant call to "Bring Back Our Girls" after 276 Nigerian schoolgirls were kidnapped by a terrorist regime. At the same time, she seems determined to remind us that — despite the challenges within and outside of our community — Blackness is not burdensome, and we, like all other human beings, have joy as a birthright, one we must work, sometimes daily, to claim. When she made us laugh — from her mom-dancing with Jimmy Fallon to her Lil Jon parody, "Turnip for What," to the College Rap with *Saturday Night Live* star Jay Pharoah — she reminded us how good it feels when you can be at home in your own skin and therefore at home in your world.

I have, over the years, been gifted with an incredible posse of homegirls. They are Black, white, Latina and Asian (and sometimes, a blend of these census-like categories). These women have my back. They were there when I jumped the broom and married my husband. They have seen me do my ugly cry and danced with me, on those sweet occasions, when we partied until night turned to day.

But the very first homegirl I ever had was named Renee Neufville. It was the early 80s and we lived in Brooklyn, then a land of

Kangol caps and Adidas sneakers, name belts, gold chains and fronts, and door knocker earrings. We were in elementary school and I knew that Renee was my homegirl because everyone said so. "What's up with your homegirl?" they'd ask. Or if I was out jumping double Dutch without Renee, they would ask, "Where your home-girl at?"

My parents were immigrants, so "home-girl" wasn't a word we used at home. It didn't just roll off of my tongue, back then. My mother and her friends, all *Latinegras* or Black Latinas, called each other, *'manita* or *comadre.* So that term, "homegirl," took some getting used to.

At the end of the day when our mothers leaned out of windows and yelled for us to come home, dinner was on the table, I would walk Renee to her house, which was around the corner and about a block away. Then she would turn around and walk me home. It seemed like there was no shortage of things for us to talk about: it was like we were, in dialogue, reading a book that had no chapters and no end. There seemed to be no place to break. We walked each other back and forth until our mothers threatened to take a switch to our behinds. In this very literal way, I came to think of a homegirl as someone with whom the soul conversation is so deep and so stirring that you keep walking each other home.

As our editor, Elisabeth Dyssegaard, and I put together this collection, I marveled at the way this anthology is less an intellectual analysis of Michelle Obama as First Lady and more a series of musings, reminiscences and pash notes to Michelle Obama as homegirl, the woman who (alongside Mindy Kaling) we all want to be friends with. Dr. Sarah Lewis connects the dots between Frederick Douglass's passion for imagery that represented African Americans with dignity and grace and the iconic portraits of Michelle O by photographers like Annie Leibovitz. Dr. Brittney Cooper ponders the mutual admiration society of our First Lady and Beyoncé. Damon Young talks about how Michelle's beauty and boldness first swayed his vote. Anyone who has ever read his Very Smart Brothas knows that his blog name is not mere hyperbole. His essay will make you think — and laugh out loud. Alicia Hall Moran and Jason Moran describe their up-close glimpses of the Obamas and how they navigate the paths of marriage, partnership, power and creativity.

Novelist Benilde Little, whose books often limn the world of the Black elite with Edith

Wharton–like knowingness, talks about Michelle Obama and authenticity. And Phillipa Soo, fresh off her Tony-nominated run as Eliza Hamilton in *Hamilton,* talks about why Michelle O is the best of wives and the best of women.

Chirlane McCray gives us her unique perspective on FLOTUS from her role as First Lady of New York City. Cathi Hanauer talks about getting married the same year as Michelle Obama — 1992 — and how she and her husband, like the President and First Lady, balanced marriage, parenthood and careers. Tiffany Dufu, author of *Drop the Ball: Achieving More by Doing Less,* muses on how Michelle Obama is perfect precisely because she's not trying to be. And Ylonda Gault Caviness shares how close so many of us feel to the First Lady in her essay, "We Go Way Back."

Rebecca Carroll weaves a powerful connection between Michelle O and Zora Neale Hurston in her essay, "She Loves Herself When She Is Laughing: Michelle Obama, Taking Down a Stereotype and Co-Creating a Presidency."

In "She Slays," Tanisha Ford talks about Michelle Obama's style and the importance of fashion in the cultural history. As Ford writes, "Style has always mattered to Black

Americans. We have been enslaved, have been denied equal rights, and have been, and continue to be, the targets of state-sanctioned and vigilante violence. Clothing is a way we reclaim our humanity, express our creativity, celebrate our roots, and forge political solidarities. We style out as a mode of survival."

Marcus Samuelsson takes us behind the scenes in his role as chef of the Obamas' first White House state dinner, but also — as an Ethiopian-born, Swedish-raised, Harlemite — talks about the importance of Michelle Obama as a role model to girls and women on a global scale. Karen Hill Anton writes to us from the countryside of Japan where she has made her home for forty years. In her essay, "The Freedom to Be Yourself," she talks about how Michelle Obama has inspired her and how her life in Japan has allowed her to live as an American first. Rebecca Carroll takes a deep look at Michelle O's sense of humor and the confidence and grace that is at its base. In her essay "Making Space," Roxane Gay explains how Michelle Obama's arc of authenticity inspires us all: "Whenever I think about Michelle Obama, I think, 'When I grow up, I want to be just like her.' I want to be that intelligent, confident, and comfortable in my own skin."

The Obamas are now preparing to leave the White House and step, for the first time in a decade, into semi-private life. For those of us who think of Michelle as more than our First Lady, it is clear that we will struggle with our goodbyes in much the same way that me and my friend Renee could not stop our dreaming and scheming for the impertinent interruptions of homework, dinner and sleep.

The goodbyes will be tough but I'm hopeful that the gratitude will be mighty and ongoing. There's a through line of thankfulness that runs through this anthology, so let me be the first to start the praise song: Thank you for inspiring us, thank you for letting us in and lifting us up. Thank you for showing us how to infuse old roles with new imagination and grace.

The writer Brené Brown writes of how essential it is to own our belonging that there should be "no more hustling for worthiness." But when race remains such a powder keg issue, this can be a hard thing even for the most affluent and educated among us to do. And yet, this reach toward confidence in our belonging is perhaps one of the most important struggles of our time. James Baldwin knew this, and it is why he once wrote that he hoped future generations of Black Americans would remember that "your crown has been bought and paid for. All you have to do is wear it." Thank you, Michelle Obama, for showing us how to wear it.

MICHELLE IN HIGH COTTON

BENILDE LITTLE

The first time I saw a picture of Michelle post 2008 inauguration I literally cried. She was featured in the Style section of the Sunday *New York Times,* dressed in that fabulous, custom-made purple dress. I was reading in bed, next to my husband who handed me the section, knowing it was then the first thing I read. I got a few lines into the story, welled up and then literally burst out crying.

"Why are you crying?" Cliff asked. By now he was used to me breaking into tears, the way some people break into song. Do you remember the way the Holly Hunter character in *Broadcast News* used to have an appointment sob daily before everyone else showed up for work? She would sit on the floor in her office, unplug her phone and sob. For no apparent reason. Me too.

"I'm just so happy. She's like me," I said. She was the first woman I'd ever seen in

28

The New York Times — or any majority media outlet — with whom I completely identified. She was part of my tribe. He looked at me, surely thinking, *She ain't really.* But my dear husband had the good sense to keep his opinion to himself. He must've understood that I knew something he didn't; an unuttered, undecipherable code of Black womanhood that he'd never be able to tune in to. It's kinda of like the way we say *gurl* to each other, but more nuanced. *Gurl* can be an appraisal, but a loving one that basically says, "I see you. You are me and I am you."

I'm not gon front, I'm not talking about *all* Black women: We are not a monolith. We have nuances and there are tribes within this tribe. Michelle is part of my tribe. In my tribe:

- We're honest with ourselves and the world around us.
- We value other women. We hold each other up with no interest in the tear down.
- We strive to achieve and keep it real for us — however that looks. There's no one size fits all.

Tracee Ellis Ross is a part of our tribe.

She shows up sans makeup and without gettin' her hair did. She gangsta raps as an alter-ego character, T-Murda — which is straight-out hilarious. She shows up on *Blackish* with her hair cornrowed and bamboo earrings, and then she shows up straight-up fashion flawless. I love what seems like her acceptance of her total self — not just as a glam actress and daughter of a superstar icon.

Holly Robinson Peete is part of the tribe, too. She went to Sarah Lawrence (as did Robin Givens — they actually had a fist fight there), did her successful sitcom stint — never playing chitlin', neck-rollin' stereotypes — found a good, smart, solid dude (an athlete, no less), had a bunch of babies, stayed married to him and does important foundation work. Props to gossip queen Wendy Williams and 80s *It girl* actress Givens, but neither of them are part of this tribe and they probably wouldn't want to be.

It might be easier to say who we are not. We're not: Glamazons who stomp around in six-inch heels, hoisting a handbag that costs a salary in some parts of the country, with somebody else's straightened hair down our backs. Publicly tearing folks down is not edifying for us. We want to look good but like ourselves with an individual twist — like Michelle rocking a J. Crew sweater with an haute couture skirt.

Pre-Michelle, the Black women in media — who weren't Halle Berry or Oprah — were either perfect pitch, high bourg or stone ghettoians (Lil' Kim), no shades or complexities as humans are. We can be round-the-way, love being with our peeps from the 'hood, be comfortable having drinks with our girls at The Mandarin Oriental, sit on museum boards, have close friendships with white girls and some of us have white husbands — all while holding on to an inner compass, not one set by someone else's judgment of what's best.

Michelle was a real hard-working professional, from a working-class South Side Chicago family, who shuttled her daughters to dance lessons and movie play dates on Saturdays. Just like I did. She looked regular — could look amazing (like in that purple sheath) or not — sometimes photographed with her hair pulled back and not in a cute chignon, but in that I-need-to-go-to-the-beauty-parlor-but-I-don't-have-the-time look. Her good Chicago friend Yvonne Davila insists that Michelle is "Real. She is you, she is me, she is everybody."

Coming from the South Side provides natives with a very specific sense of place. Chicago is an extremely racially polarized city and Michelle has that "thing" people from the South Side have. I have a good friend who grew up there and she says, "It's hard to get that South Side out of us." I asked her to explain it and this is what I've gathered: folks from there have a defiant grounded-ness; a resoluteness perhaps born in the Black Belt (Alabama and Mississippi) where most Black Chicagoans came from.

The Black Belt had the largest cash crop, cotton, and those enslaved there, it has been said, were treated most harshly. (To be clear, that's like saying the whippings were every day instead of six days a week.)

The South Side attitude of togetherness was borne of being excluded from much of the city's political power for so long. When a Black man, Harold Washington, was finally elected mayor in 1983, Black people there were literally dancing in the streets.

People from the South Side have a tell-it-like-it-is way about themselves. Now, don't get it twisted. It's not all Kumbaya togetherness. There was and is a sharp class division there, too (although everybody Black was down with the election of Harold Washington). There are the generations of Chicagoans who are college-educated folks; some who are so light-skinned you gotta look hard to discern any African heritage. In the early days, that segment filled selective groups like Jack and Jill, the Links, some Greek-lettered organizations.

Michelle's dad worked fixing boilers in the city's water department and her mom went to work as a secretary after her children entered elementary school. The Robinsons were not even close to qualifying for membership in the Black bourgeoisie and from all appearances that wasn't a goal. Her family, like mine, stressed education and wanted their children to be free, to have choices about how they would make a living — to have a career as opposed to a job. The Robinsons stressed solidly middle-class values, not social strata aspirations. Our neighborhoods were Black — up and down the spectrum.

I have watched how Michelle navigated the world of her childhood as she took the world stage. I greedily gobbled up anything she said about that world. I looked for anything I could find about her girlfriends — any bit of info that would provide insight into more of who she is. I did look up two of her best friends on Facebook and found that both of them are real regular. The home décor in one house featured chain store furniture and curtains, not drapes, in the living room. Real, real.

"One of the most interesting aspects of the Obamas' ascendency is that neither one of them is the product of this approval-dependent world of relentless obligation, prayerful duty and punishing well-scrubbed-ness . . . And since both of Michelle Obama's parents were working class, it's doubtful that they would have considered the hefty fees and consuming time commitments a priority, even assuming they'd have met the more social-climbing criteria that a number of such [elite] clubs emphasize," Professor Patricia Williams wrote in *The Daily Beast.*[1]

Although the term "South Side" is thrown around like a blanket for "Black," for the 'hood, it's quite diverse. There are middle-class, working-class and affluent pockets. While geographically Hyde Park is only about a mile from where Michelle grew up, it might as well be another state. Hyde Park is fancy and stately and has always been an island — home of brainy University of Chicago. Michelle told a reporter from *MORE* magazine: "As a black kid on the South Side, the University of Chicago was a foreign entity to me." She said as a young person she had never set foot on the campus.[2]

"All the buildings have their backs to the community. The university didn't think kids like me existed, and I certainly didn't want anything to do with that place."[3]

A Chicago friend, Cindy Moelis, says Michelle wanted a house — a big house with a big yard. "Barack wanted his family to be comfortable, but he would have been satisfied with three spoons, a fork, and a dish," says an acquaintance who talked to him often about the matter. "It was an issue for her." She got to indulge in her dream house — in Hyde Park/Kenwood, a $1.65 million, six-bedroom, three-story Georgian revival mansion with a wine cellar and dark wood paneling — when Barack's convention speech in 2004 sent his memoir onto best-seller lists, and the couple suddenly had money. It is where she and Barack settled and made a close group of friends who seemed to be like them — accomplished doctors, lawyers, entrepreneurs who all seemed "down," not interested in membership in the established Black elite — even though they all had qualifying credentials.

Their good friend and political godmother, Valerie Jarrett, is Black Chicago royalty and referred to as Barack's secret weapon. Valerie, who grew up going to her family's home on Martha's Vineyard, introduced that Black Bourgeois mecca to Michelle and Barack. The writer Touré wrote a piece for *New York* magazine about the ritual gathering (the generational ownership of homes on the island) and, in his view, the myriad criteria for being welcomed there. While trying to unlock the mystery of the island's attractions and assess the Vineyard's suitability as a vacation spot for our new First Family, he spoke to one anonymous, snobby, long-time islander who reportedly questioned Michelle Obama's place in the group's hierarchy, referring to the First Lady as a "ghetto girl." The actual quote: "[Michelle Obama] is basically a ghetto girl. She grew up in the same place Jennifer Hudson did. She hasn't reached out to the social community of Washington."[4]

I know. Really? *Clutch the damn pearls.*

Fortunately, there was a loud outcry at such a statement, including from those in the established old guard. They got together and wrote a letter to the *Vineyard Gazette* and complained that Touré had portrayed them as a bunch of racist snobs. He stood by what he had written, maintaining that the article was written in admiration, not condemnation — and he had the unnamed

36

source on tape. I had no problem believing that someone had made this comment. As an "outsider" who started going to the Vineyard in the early 80s and returned twenty years later (when my daughter begged us to rent our own house so she didn't have to keep sponging off her friend's grandparents), I'd been asked: How long have you been coming? Code: Are you old or new? The area of Oak Bluffs is considered "our town" by the old guard and anyone new is socially X-rayed. However, I know lots of the old guard who are lovely and welcoming; and it's become much more democratic, and crowded, in the last 25-plus years. The small-town feeling is gone, and with it some of the possessiveness, even as many of the homeowners complain about all the new people.

As a Black person with a lot of the same accoutrements as the elite, it can be an intricate dance of expressing your true self, holding on to that "ghetto girl" while travelling so far from your origins. Being in worlds that have no understanding of or exposure to where you're from — the real, not the stereotype — can be exhausting and sometimes lonely. Michelle seems to flawlessly navigate these uncharted, sometimes hostile terrains.

Michelle never responded publicly to the "ghetto girl" comment, but I would've loved to have been a fly on the wall when she did so in private. I'm sure there was at least a mention of it among her girls and maybe even with her mama. Marian Robinson clearly don't take no mess, or as the old folks say: No tea for the fever. In other words, she seems just like the kind of straight-talking, no-foolishness-tolerating Black mother I had.

Michelle has ruling-class education credentials — those worshipped by many in the Black elite — yet she was far from that. She wears her working-class roots as easily as she wears Narciso. But, when she talked about having shared a room with her brother, Craig, a partition between twin beds providing their only privacy while her parents slept in the living room, I stood back in awe of her. How did she do that? How did she find her balance at Princeton, when that ruling-class environment crushed middle-class kids of color?

"At Princeton in the 1980s, she had remained somewhat aloof from the white students, partly by preference and partly because Blacks weren't welcome at the exclusive eating clubs that dominated campus social life. The family of her first roommate, a Southern white woman, had protested to the university administration because their daughter had been assigned to room with a black person," Geraldine Brooks wrote in *More* magazine.[5]

Many years ago, I went to a post–football game party held by one of Princeton's exclusive eating clubs. The Ivy is the most selective of the select and it was literally painful to be there. I was 24 and felt as if I had a neon sign on my forehead, but I was utterly invisible to all the plastered white faces. My boyfriend at the time (who had been a member) and the guys balancing trays of pigs in a blanket and cocktails were the only other Black folks — or people of color — in the room. He was a lovely guy who had been a scholar and three-letter athlete, and he was revered and very comfortable in this world of old-line WASPS.

Michelle has talked about not always feeling at home at Princeton. In a *Washington Post* piece, Robin Givhan, a Princeton alum, quotes Michelle: "My experiences at Princeton have made me far more aware of my 'Blackness' than ever before . . . I have found that at Princeton no matter how liberal and open-minded some of my White professors and classmates try to be toward me, I sometimes feel like a visitor on campus; as if I really don't belong. Regardless of the circumstances under which I interact with Whites at Princeton, it often seems as if, to them, I will always be Black first and a student second."[6]

She's said she had a similar feeling at Harvard Law School, but she became active in the Black student union and that helped see her through. "The truth is that if Princeton hadn't found my brother as a basketball recruit and if I hadn't seen that he could succeed on a campus like that, it never would have occurred to me to apply to that school — never."[7]

As someone who has written fairly extensively about class divisions among Black folk and who, during my time at Howard University, struggled with finding a place of belonging once I became aware that there was such a thing as social class, I found Michelle nothing short of amazing. At Northwestern, where I went to graduate school, it was another Black student who introduced class and color discussions among our white friends and classmates. And incidentally, in the early 80s, they had no idea what she was talking about when she constantly referred to herself as being "high yella," and the social hierarchy based on such.

I grew up in Newark, with two working

parents. My dad worked on the assembly line at General Motors, and my mom was a nurse's aide. In my unsophistication, I thought poor and working-class people only came in shades of brown. I thought that rich people only came in one shade even if all white people weren't rich. I assumed that anyone who had generational wealth and higher education was white. Yes, there were a few teachers in my neighborhood, but that was it, in terms of Black folks with a college education.

At Howard, I had an apartment off-campus with two roommates and my dad had bought me a car to make it easier to commute from my place in Maryland. I didn't know that the off-campus apartment and the car set me up to look like a member of the Black elite. Rich girls lived like this. So when other students asked me questions like: "What does your father do?" or even more strange, "What did your grandfather do?" I was completely baffled. *You mean what does he do when he comes home from work?* I literally didn't even understand the question. But members of the Black elite tribe do.

This presumption that I was one of "them" set me on a path of questioning myself, obsessing about my image, and taking lots of paths — friends, boyfriends and therapy — before I found my north star. Color and class are often entwined — again something of which I was totally (and blissfully) ignorant. I was two semesters in before I realized that there was some kind of currency placed on lighter skin. I remember the early spring day the fuse lit and my blissful ignorance was shattered.

When the crocuses open, the Howard yard swells with a composite of Q-dogs in front of their fraternity tree, an impromptu step show likely; the Ubiquity folk — natural-haired (before everyone was), incense-smelling, dirty backpacks — dissecting Fanon on a bench in front of Douglass Hall; the Five Percenters in their bow ties and their White-man-is-the-Devil theories near the Blackburn student center. There were the Fine Arts folk-dancers in sinewy bodies, Danskin bodysuits and flowing print-colored skirts between Crampton Auditorium and Douglass. There were the BAPS; the Nupes (Kappa fraternity boys); the urban kids from the Bronx and Philly, Detroit and Oakland; the oreos from places like Seattle and Cheyenne, Wyoming. There was me, standing between the side of Douglass Hall and Crampton Auditorium. I was with my friend Lori, a D.C. native and my

Indian guide. She was an expert dissector of class and color in Washington.

Suddenly the conversation and the music and dancing and poetry seemed to pause and a phalanx of girls walking five abreast — hair bouncing and behaving like an advertisement for Clairol — crossed the pathway. I noticed the guys stop what they were doing to observe them. The girls' skin tones were between Paula Patton and Beyoncé. I looked at the girls, seemingly oblivious to the attention, smiling and laughing among each other and there was the ding. *Oh they're considered special because of their coloring.* I was surprised and confused and then mad. No one had told me about this. Where I was raised the Black is Beautiful doctrine of the 1960s was still part of the zeitgeist. I wonder if Michelle knew about this strange color/classism when she was growing up. I wonder how she'd reacted, if she'd been as shaken as I had been.

To her Princeton classmate Beverly Thomison-Sadia, Michelle seemed unusually sure of herself. "Michelle always arrived at her own opinion. It wasn't the women's position; it wasn't the black position. Michelle would take all the information and process it through her experience, her beliefs, her value system, and she would arrive at the Michelle Robinson position or opinion."[8]

I think it's easier to bypass the notion of colorism and the notion of the Black elite at elite (white) institutions. At a place like Howard or Spelman and Morehouse, it's in your face.

She did have a best friend at Princeton, a Jamaican-born daughter of two doctors, who died of cancer at the age 25. Michelle was with her when she took her last breath, and it was apparently one of the most devastating experiences of her life. When you're a fly in the buttermilk, often race trumps class. Howard Taylor, then the director of the school's Center for African American Studies, says Michelle was "wrestling with the question of just how to be black at Princeton. Do you socialize pretty exclusively with black students or do you try to integrate and associate relatively equally with white students?" Michelle eventually "came down on the side of hanging not exclusively black but for the most part black," Taylor said.[9]

I wonder what Michelle thought of the Black kids from the tony private schools and Jack and Jill. Maybe like me she didn't think about them because she didn't know that they existed. Doubtful, considering that one of her best friends from high school was Santita Jackson, daughter of Jesse, one of Martin Luther King's comrades. While the Jacksons are not officially, technically Black elite, they are Black civil rights royalty. And it's been reported that Michelle spent so much time at the Jackson household, "Jesse could've charged her rent." (Santita, who came to Howard just as I was graduating, is godmother to Malia.)[10]

In August 1966, when Michelle was a preschooler, her parents — like all of Chicago and the nation — were witness to the violent reaction of whites to a Martin Luther King–led march through a white Chicago neighborhood to bring attention to the substandard living conditions of urban Black Chicagoans. Many local whites threw bricks (one hit King in the head), knives were thrown at protesters, cars were vandalized and set afire, cops were punched. King said: "I have seen many demonstrations in the south but I have never seen anything so hostile and so hateful as I've seen here today."[11]

Michelle came of age at the tail end of Black Power, which might explain her supreme self-confidence in being exactly who she is. But let's face it: The Black elite with its obsession with class and color had

45

to touch her life at some point. She is a dark-skinned woman without "classically" beautiful features and no social provenance. A very smart friend of mine once said that Barack wouldn't win because America wasn't ready for a dark-skinned woman in the White House. I vehemently disagreed with her and when he won, she happily admitted that she'd been wrong.

In 2007, Michelle told *Vogue* magazine: "I say this not to be modest, but there are so many young people who could be me. There's nothing magical about my background. I am not a super genius. I had good parents and some good teachers and some decent breaks, and I work hard. Every other kid I knew could have been me, but they got a bad break and didn't recover. It's like I tell the young people I talk to: The difference between success and failure in our society is a very slim margin. You almost have to have that perfect storm of good parents, self-esteem, and good teachers. It's a lot, which is why Barack and I believe so passionately about investing in education and strengthening institutions."[12]

Thing is, Michelle is like so many of us and she knows it. She was raised by striving, working-class Black parents. During the time we grew up, pretty much all Black parents were strivers and I don't mean that in a grubbing, social climbing way — no, it was an achievement climb. It was about uplift, but not emulating white folks. The dream was that we would hold on to the values we learned in those Black neighborhoods and then we'd go out and conquer, but we wouldn't "forget our raising." That didn't quite happen or it didn't happen for enough of us; we did not all hold on to our essential selves. Michelle did. She brought her mama with her to the White House, which means she brought her home with her; she and Barack have the same friends and brought them along, too. It's hard being oneself under a microscope and the miracle of Michelle is that she seems to have always held on to her authentic self — with lots of her middle name, LaVaughn — holding center, unlike me who traveled a path to get back to my authentic Neal.

There's something enviable (now) about women who don't spend a lot of time looking in the rearview mirror. Michelle went away to school and law school but moved back to her hometown and settled into her professional life, married, and became a mother all while within a five-mile radius. There's a lot to be said for that. Her husband has adopted her hometown as his.

Never any fight about which parents to spend the holidays with. Her brother Craig sums her up: "Michelle doesn't like to play games and it's not because she hates to lose, it's because she wants everybody to win."[13]

Michelle resonates for us on a deeply personal level. She's given us permission to be ourselves, on a national stage, to be proud of our Blackness, our realness, our humble beginnings, our regular-ness, our greatness. To not be perfect and to not even have that as a goal, because she's smart enough to understand that perfection is its own prison.

When we look back on the Obamas' stay at 1600, as fantastical and far-fetched as his presidency seemed to be eight years ago, it was as real as Michelle is. A dark-skinned, working-class Black girl marries a biracial, Black-identified intellectual equal who ends up becoming the leader of the free world. They raised their young daughters into young womanhood under a spotlight with not one whiff of bad public behavior. It's a story even the best of us wouldn't have dared to dream, much less write.

CRUSHING ON MICHELLE: OR THE UNAPOLOGETIC POWER OF BLACKNESS

DAMON YOUNG

The first time I heard Barack Obama's name was in 2004. I was a teacher at Wilkinsburg High School (located in a Pittsburgh-adjacent suburb) and one of my colleagues burst into my classroom gushing about him, having seen his keynote the night before at the Democratic National Convention. He even claimed this guy would be president one day.

Unfortunately, America had already given me a healthy and practical skepticism of the type of Black people White people gush about, so I smiled, thought "Whatever, man" and kept putting numbers in Grade Quick.

Barack Obama? I thought, Did he even pronounce it right? That sounds like a stage name. Or the alias of a Black superhero. A poor man's King T'challa.

Still, I kept his name stored away, and felt my interest pique a bit later when Common namedropped him on a remix of Jadakiss's "Why."

> Why is Bush acting like he trying to get
> Osama
> Why don't we impeach him and elect
> Obama

This was enough for me to start a sincere investigation. Who is this mysteriously named man? Where is he from? Is he biracial or just a light-skinned brotha with two light-skinned Black parents? What is he about? Is he for real? Can he hoop?

Each of these questions had easy-to-determine answers that could be found with a 10-second jaunt to Google. But the best and most honest way for me to find each of the answers I desired involved a follow-up question:

"Who is he married to?"

And then I learned about Michelle.

I read up on her background and her resume. Her Chicago roots. Her sociology degree from Princeton, where she graduated cum laude, and her J.D. from Harvard Law School when she was 24. (24!)

I learned about her mother, Marian Robinson, and her father, Fraser Robinson III, a man whose battle with multiple sclerosis inspired Michelle to excel academically. I learned that I — a basketball maven who makes a point of being aware of the relatively minute number of Black Division-1 coaches — actually knew about her brother. I was very well acquainted with then-Brown University head coach Craig Robinson.

I found out about Barack and Michelle's history. How he pursued her in the type of persistent, Darius Lovehall from *Love Jones*-esque manner that became a cute anecdote since it worked and would have been a scary story about a Chicago creeper if it didn't. I learned about their first date; a trip to see *Do The Right Thing,* which is either the best or the worst choice for a first date movie ever. And then I met Sasha and Malia, the two beautiful daughters who somehow manage to be doppelgangers of both their parents.

And, I also saw *her.* And I couldn't (and, to be honest, still can't) wrap my mind around the fact that this woman had an actual chance of being the First Lady.

No offense to any of the wives of the presidents before President Obama — all lovely, gracious, and exemplary women — but damn! I was used to First Ladies being, well, professional First Ladies. Nice, grandmotherly white ladies who belonged to

Silver Sneakers and shared houses in Florida with women named "Rose" and "Blanche." Not statuesque and preternaturally attractive brown-skinned women with grace and style and sex appeal and swag. She was the real life version of the characters Angela Bassett and Gina Torres have spent the last decade of their careers playing. The type of woman who'd walk into a board meeting or a yoga class or a Trader Joe's or a Friday happy hour on U Street in D.C. and make you instinctively straighten your posture, tighten your gut, and settle your gait. Because you knew that in order to have any type of meaningful interaction with her, you'd need to have your shit together. And you desperately wanted to have that shit together — or, at least, do a convincing job convincing her you had that shit together — because you desperately wanted to approach her, to talk to her, to know her, and for her to know and be impressed by and remember you. She was a level-lifter. An aspiration. An ambition. The woman you'd want to meet if you planned on taking over the world, together.

And then my tepid and halting support for Barack Obama became a fervent following. How could I not throw all of my chips in with a Black man who had the wherewithal, the foresight, the wisdom, and the *game* (Yes. The game.) to marry her? If he found a way to convince this amazing woman to accept his hand and have his children, he's exactly the type of man I want to be my president.

Now before I continue, let me make a couple things clear. I'm in no way suggesting that a politician must be married (or straight) to be an impactful one worthy of support. Nor would I dream of implying that if a Black politician happens to be married, they must be married to a Black person. There are myriad examples of brilliant and committed Black people who've chosen partners who are not Black, and perhaps even more examples of substandard Black lawmakers who married within their race.

But I can't deny my truth, which is a truth shared by many other Black people who shared my skepticism. Yes, we eventually fell in love with Barack Obama. We bought the pins and the pens and stuck the bumper stickers on our windshields (and, if we didn't happen to have a car, our bookbags). We made the phone calls and canvassed the neighborhoods, attempting to register people everywhere from family BBQs and Omega Psi Phi boat rides to beauty salons and barbershops. We attended the rallies. Shit, we had pre-rally happy hours and post-rally potlucks. We had watch parties and tweet-ups for his debates, treating them the same way we treat *Scandal* season premieres and the BET Awards. We bought and rocked the T-shirts with his face on them. Which, in hindsight, was probably rather creepy. But we did it anyway. We even adopted Joe Biden!

But Michelle was the conduit. Michelle was the one who signaled that it was right and safe for us to do all of these things. Essentially, the anti-coal mine canary. She was our litmus test. The final and most important exam Barack had to pass. We weren't just voting for Barack. We desired to see Barack *and* Michelle (and Sasha and Malia) in the White House. To be paraded and honored around the world. Because while Barack was the rock star, the headliner, it was Michelle and not her husband who we fell in love with first.

Of course, much of this love was mined from the symbolic nature of the Obama family's ascendance and prominence. And we made no bones about it; we wanted this unambiguously Black family to be America's first family. (If you asked a typical Black Obama supporter in 2007 or 2008 if they only supported him because he was Black, the most likely answer would be "Of course!") It was a cathartic desire; one mined out of the historic context of the Black American in America, a latent sense of and want for validation, an acknowledgement of the psychic impact this would have on America (Black America, specifically), and a very real want for America's HNIC to be an actual nigga. Also, many of us (myself included) took a particular glee from the thought of historically prominent and morally minor racists like Bull Conner and George Wallace and all the people who believed our parents and uncles and aunts and grandparents and us weren't worthy of full citizenship doing 1,000 revolutions per minute in their graves.

But, when speaking specifically of Michelle (and speaking from a heterosexual Black man's perspective), this love — this cavernous reservoir of positive feeling — was largely aspirational. And for the first time in recent memory, these aspirations were centered in reality. Before her, the benchmark romantic mates for Black men were fictional characters (i.e., Claire Huxtable), attractive actresses who played desirable fictional characters so well that we projected a perfect woman status on them (i.e., Nia Long, Regina King, and Halle Berry), blaxploitation stars (i.e., Pam Grier), hosts of MTV and BET shows that aired in the 90s (i.e., Ananda Lewis or Rachel Stuart) or former members of Destiny's Child. None of these women, however, were realistically attainable. Because while some of them are very real people, the image they projected congealed with our own invented projections of them, creating perfect woman proxies that existed in a space between our imaginations and our realities.

Michelle Obama, however, was *real*. While Black Americans collectively saw her and saw our sisters and cousins and aunts and moms, we (Black men) saw her and saw our classmates and our neighbors; our coworkers and our colleagues. We saw the woman we wanted to approach, to court, to date, to commit to, to marry, and to start a family and grow old with, even if we didn't actually realize we wanted to do any of those things before we saw her. We saw a regular Black chick; but with "regular Black" being a compliment — the best compliment — instead of a pejorative.

And this, the appeal of the First Lady's "regular Blackness," cannot be overstated. She wasn't from Turks and Caicos; she was from Chicago. The same South Side immortalized in songs from Common and Kanye and name dropped whenever racists want to dog whistle a point about Black-on-Black crime. She didn't possess what's commonly and disturbingly referred to as "good hair." Her hair was full and stylish and healthy, of course. But it was Black hair, the type of hair that communicated to us all that she knew what her "kitchen" was, was very well acquainted with the nap, and had a back-and-forth relationship with hot combs. And, the lean and athletic Michelle was also blessed with a curvy behind that I'd totally call a "bubble," a "big booty" or even a "fat ass" if I wasn't attempting to be respectful of the First Lady. She wasn't the type of beautiful we'd usually see on the covers of *Vogue* and *Cosmopolitan.* But she possessed the beauty shared by the women in our families and the girls in high school and the women at Urban League Young Professionals general body meetings we crushed on. It was a beauty specific to Blackness that wasn't a specifically Black beauty. Because it was impervious to qualification. She wasn't stunning for a Black woman. She was a woman whose undeniably Black features made her stunning.

It's still far too early to accurately assess the "Obama Effect" on Black America. It'll take decades to be able to fully rate and measure the cultural impact of the Obama family's eight-year-long stint in the White House. It's even too soon to tease out and efficiently deconstruct easy-to-determine stats like Black marriage rates and HBCU enrollment. There's just not enough of a sample size to distinguish an actual trend — and the Obama's connection to that trend — from statistical noise.

That said, I possess a few theories on the Obamas' level of permeation and influence on our cultural zeitgeist; thoughts with no actual factual basis but instead determined from a mélange of feeling, anecdote, experience, observation, and conversation at happy hours after three Honey Jack and ginger ales.

I think the Obamas have helped shepherd in both a collective embrace of unapologetic Blackness and a new generation of Black writers, academics, thinkers, activists, and pundits unconcerned with the White gaze. I think the photos of President Obama playing basketball provided validation for all the middle-aged Black men who have (1) said the first thing they'd do if elected president is organize the best pick-up games ever (like what President Obama did) and who (2) catch shit from their wives and children for regularly hooping in sweatpants and tucked-in white shirts. Because if President Obama does it too, it's officially cool. I think we're going to see a boom of Black babies named Barack, Sasha, and Malia. I think the light-skinned Black man, who jokingly was considered to be "out of style," will continue to experience a renaissance. I think rappers will continue to find and invent unique words to rhyme with Obama. I think the already stale and abjectly false stereotype of Black people not appreciating intellect and academic achievement will die a slow and painful death. I think Washington, D.C., has officially replaced Atlanta as the Mecca for Black America. And since brunch is the preferred meal of choice for Black Washingtonians, I think it'll officially replace the cookout as the peak Blackest meal.

But mostly I think the onslaught of criticism Michelle has received pretty much nonstop from Whites who just haven't been able to accept that a woman like her is considered beautiful — snide comments and just outright nasty remarks about everything from her body and her facial features to her height and her gait — caused us to circle the wagons around her. Because she's our fucking First Lady so show some damn respect. And also because the insults about Michelle's commonly and perfectly Black features were not-so-subtle shots at ours, too. If they believed the things they said about this woman, they felt the same way about us. And I believe that defense of Michelle helped many of us acknowledge, accept, confront, and attempt to alter some of the more unsavory and unflattering latent beliefs and subconscious feelings we possessed about our skin and our noses and our eyes and our hair.

It's a legacy I'm amazed by when I think of kids like my 9-year-old niece and 11-year-old nephew. While those older vividly remember a time when the thought of a Black president and Black First Lady was, if not quite absurd, unrealistic (and still surreal, struggling at times to wrap our minds around the whole idea), for children this age, this is literally *all they know.* They have no conception, no recollection, no *idea* of existing in an America without a Black president. They will have racial and cultural baggage, like we all do. But they will have less of it. All my niece knows is Sasha and Malia and Michelle — Black girls who look like her and a Black woman who looks like her mom — when she turns on CNN or picks up a newspaper or is in line at Giant Eagle and glances at the magazines in the aisle or is asked to research the First Family for a project at school. Perhaps she's not old enough yet to fully process what she's seen and heard, but she *has* seen and heard her mother and grandmother and aunts and uncles defend Michelle Obama's Blackness. And now she knows Blackness — and all the beautifully Black things specific to her — is worthy of defense.

Michelle Obama, our First First Lady, did that.

The Composer and the Brain: A Conversation about Music, Marriage, Power, Creativity, Partnership . . . and the Obamas

ALICIA HALL MORAN AND JASON MORAN

Alicia:

I first met Michelle Obama when I was understudying the role of Bess in *Porgy and Bess* on Broadway. After the show was over, after the curtain call, we stayed on stage in our costumes. She came up to each of us and hugged every one of us, regardless of whether we were the star of the show or a backstage hand. Her love and support were gold. Celebrities (people with much less important things to do than run the world) send the vibe, too often, that they can't be bothered with you. Michelle Obama *can* be bothered with you.

Jason:

Both the President and the First Lady are so present, so generous. For the groundbreaking of the African American museum, I played a song. Then after, we all went to the White House. The Obamas came out to meet people and it was a big crowd. Someone from the staff took me by the arm and said, "You need to get to the front."

Michelle said, "Elizabeth [Alexander] just told us about you and we really love you." Then Barack comes right behind her and he says, "Yes, I really liked that song."

He said, "Michelle really does the listening to music, but I'm going to find that song."

I was thinking, *he's bullshitting me about that song.*

He said, "You think I'm lying. I'm not lying to you." He reached into his pocket and took out this piece of paper. It was just a white card and written on it, very small, was: "Jason Moran, I Like the Sunrise." He showed it to me and he said, "I'm looking for that song."

It's very hard to be genuine all the time, but somehow they shine in these personal interactions.

Alicia:

He also said, "Those kids must be good piano players." He mentioned our kids and it's like, they're really showing you, how artful and connected they are.

Jason:

When we got married, we were lucky that there were a number of couples who could be models for us. Our parents were the easiest and primary examples. My parents stayed married until my mother passed a year after we were married. Alicia's parents are still married. Once I left Texas and got to New York, I realized it was more common to meet people who don't stick together. So we made it a point to find other people who we thought were models. One example was Fred Wilson and Whitfield Lovell. I feel that they have been great models of partnership, friendship and being artists together.

One thing my grandmother said when we got married is: Make sure you communicate. That's what you really learn in a marriage to admit when you're lost and when you're wrong. I'm still trying to learn that lesson.

That's what makes me cherish Alicia more

and more. I can cut off. Alicia is able to pull what really needs to be said out of us.

Alicia:
Isn't that great? What he's talking about is me persecuting him with my nagging. But *he* can make a poem of it.

Jason:
Like the Obamas, especially when he was a senator and then later on the campaign trail, the distance has always been built in. As a musician, I started going on the road in college. Then after school, I was on the road too.

We managed it in our relationship, but nobody prepares you for having children and navigating the distance and travel in your work. I was always indebted to Alicia for holding it down at home and raising our kids when I needed to be on the road. So when the opportunity came for her to tour as Bess in the national company of *Porgy and Bess,* I said, "Yes, I can be here for nine months. I'm *supposed* to be here."

My touring life is something that I'm still wrestling with. As our kids get older, I have to build a different system because this won't sustain in a healthy way forever. One of the ways I'm trying to wean myself off of the idea that I have to be on the road is in considering how potent jazz is for Black people and that we need more jazz, here in America.

At each various stage of our marriage, I've said to Alicia, "What was I doing before we were married?" The good and the bad, this is so much better than what existed beforehand.

I call Alicia the brain. When we were in Venice last summer, I posted a photo of the two of us and I said, "Plotting with the Brain on Your Behalf."

The Brain is pretty literal. I met Alicia as she graduated from Barnard. What she brought into my life was an intellectual component that was totally absent. None of my friends were discussing music in a way that brought in place and the landscapes that the music emerges from, what are the codes and meanings. She had this amazingly rigorous comprehension of not only Black music, but German music and French music and what it means to culture and society.

I was learning how to do the music, but I

wasn't necessarily concerned with why I was making it. Alicia is the one who said, "You need to turn that around. If you turn this around sooner, you'll be ahead of nearly everyone else because it's clear that none of your friends are thinking about this."

And when I think of the conversations we've had over the years, I think about the conversations that Michelle and Barack must have in private. How he applies what Michelle says and how I apply all the things I've heard Alicia say. How do people apply the knowledge or criticism they've been given privately?

Also Alicia and I are extremely aware, which I'm pretty sure that Barack and Michelle are too, of the people who took their hand, the people who are not mentioned in any article or book. People who took their hand and showed them something and didn't tell them how to apply it, but just stepped back and let them transact on this knowledge over and over again.

Their level of achievement doesn't happen by just being a good student. Somebody teaches you how to learn, somebody teaches you how to be around other people, how and when to be demanding, and they've somehow really gotten the lesson and used it.

Alicia:

Something Jason always says is, "You don't know when it will come back to you." You give the gift and you don't know when it will come back. But you give of yourself, and you earn that "time to get my blessings bucket" and someone will smell you. You have the fresh clean scent of having done something for someone else.

I like the way the Obamas represent a reaching towards what I call, "the best that is at our disposal." From the way she dresses to where they send their girls to school, it is a constant reminder of *we can* and *you can.* "I'm going to wear this J. Crew dress. I'm not going to send my kids to boarding school in the French countryside. They'll go where other girls in D.C. go."

A large contingent of us are still in love with them because they dared greatly. She said, "You could be president."

Jason:

I wonder what it was like when they first said it out loud, to each other.

Alicia:

They dared to say it. Then they tried with humility. The humility with which they approached the bid for the presidency was an example to the nation. I wouldn't call what Donald Trump did daring or trying; it's like he's just hurtling with velocity at the highest office in the nation.

Jason:

You never get the feeling with the Obamas that they are starved for attention. They shine the light broadly on the whole community.

Alicia:

Talk about making room in that House. I have now shaken hands with Michelle Obama and Barack Obama more than I did with the president of my college or the dean of my music conservatory.

Michelle Obama is as good as it gets and that's a fact.

Jason:
That is a fact.

Alicia:

She has achieved what we Black people have really taken personally, what Maya Angelou called "the dream of the slave." It makes living in a contemporary society very easy. It's easier to be brave in our era when possibility is modeled the way that that couple has. Think of what we once endured, just a few generations ago: lashings for just lifting your face when the master spoke, lashings for eating an extra piece of bread, lashings for covering for a sister who has pregnancy pain and can't lift a chair. The lashings, all those lashings. Our great-great grandparents saw this and endured those and now the dream is here. We have him and her.

Jason:

They are just getting started.

Alicia:

She's had three careers in one lifetime and she's not even an old woman yet.

Jason:

Alicia and I have understood that our greater power lies in the community being given power. The more people have power, that collective power would seep out farther and wider and become a way stronger wave than anything we might do individually.

Now there's a history behind what we've done and continue to do, this is a wave that can't be stopped now. It's building momentum.

The world doesn't yet know the scope of what Alicia has to offer. I don't think she does, either. But I know by the virtue of the conversations we have every morning and every night. The potency with which she addresses every thought is almost frightening.

When Alicia is discouraged, I think she thinks, "Well, I don't have a model for what I'm trying to do." I can look to a Duke Ellington or a Herbie Hancock in the jazz pantheon. She maintains that she's looking for something that doesn't exist or been exhibited in the popular world. But I'm watching Alicia, over the past 18 months, sit at the piano and write her songs and find the ideas in these songs.

Alicia:
Which brings us back to Michelle Obama. To accept that you will be judged is actually the job that the First Lady signs up for. I see how she threads her power through what

Ragnar Kjartansson, Scenes from Western Culture, Dinner (Jason Moran and Alicia Hall Moran)*, 2015 © Ragnar Kjartansson; courtesy of the artist, Luhring Augustine, New York, and i8 Gallery, Reykjavik.*

could have been a limited role of being judged all day long.

It's not a small role. It's an all-encompassing twenty-four-hour judgment on your future, your past and your present; your children, their present and their futures. It's everything and you're always dressing in the mirror of public engagement.

But she threads her power through these things and what she does is she reverses the gaze. She makes sure that while the world is looking at her, that she extends her gaze to the children and to the elders, to the craftsmen and the artists, to a whole range of people who had never been seen in that way before. She reversed the gaze.

LADY O AND KING BEY

BRITTNEY COOPER

The mutual girl crush that Michelle Obama and Beyoncé share is a serendipitous study in twenty-first-century Black girlhood, womanhood and ladyhood. In 2009, Beyoncé performed Etta James's classic song "At Last" at one of the inauguration balls for President Obama. Coupled with the President's professed admiration for Beyoncé's husband, Jay-Z, it seemed that the Obamas were kind of like the well-heeled, older brother and sister doppelgangers of Hip Hop's First Couple. Through the President's two terms, the romance has continued. In 2011, the First Lady partnered with Beyoncé as part of her Let's Move! campaign to combat childhood obesity. By this point in the President's first term, Mrs. Obama had made her mark as mom-in-chief, as fashion icon, and as a loving, playful, dancing advocate for the health of the nation's children.

74

In many respects, Mrs. Obama epitomizes the triumph of the project of respectability that consumed Black women organizers at the turn of the twentieth century. Late nineteenth- and early twentieth-century "race women" had hoped in the words of Harvard historian Evelyn Brooks Higginbotham that an "emphasis on respectable behavior [would contest] the plethora of negative stereotypes by introducing alternative images of black women."[1] With her Ivy League education, two-parent upbringing, traditional marriage to an Ivy League–educated brother, and two beautiful, well-behaved daughters, Michelle Obama represents more than the race women who occupied the public sphere before her could ever have dreamed. When she declared herself mom-in-chief to the chagrin of many white feminists who felt that she should "lean in," many Black women celebrated. For once, African American motherhood would be center stage in American politics in a celebratory manner. As mom-in-chief, Michelle Obama could correct decades-long stereotypes of Black women as neglectful parents and money-grubbing welfare queens. Even as these stereotypes persist as an animating force in right-wing policies in the form of ugly dog whistles about "handouts" and "personal responsibility," a visible and credible counter narrative now exists. In a world in which Black women were always treated as women but never as *ladies,* a Black woman becoming the icon of American ladyhood is a triumph of the hopes and dreams of all those race ladies of old.

Thus, Michelle Obama's vocal admiration for pop superstar Beyoncé is nothing if not curious. I'd venture to say that most grown Black women and the girls who will become them someday have an inner Beyoncé. Inner Beyoncé is a sexy chanteuse, whose milkshake brings all the boys to the yard. Inner Beyoncé might have Michelle Obama reminding her hubby Barack that she upgraded *him,* not the other way around. The curiosity is not that Michelle Obama has an inner Beyoncé; it is rather that this quintessence of twenty-first-century Black ladyhood admits to it.

Once asked who she would be if she could be anyone other than herself, Michelle Obama replied, "Beyoncé." And Beyoncé has embraced this relationship with mutual admiration and affection. It is Beyoncé who grew up in an upper-middle-class family in Houston, while Michelle Obama grew up a generation earlier in a working-class family on Chicago's South Side. It is Michelle

Obama who took a chance on a lawyer with little money and less professional rank than her, while Beyoncé married the former drug dealer turned rap music mogul Jay-Z. Still, because Beyoncé makes her money through not only her considerable vocal talent but also her consummate beauty and sex appeal, she invokes a different social genealogy of Black womanhood than the one from which Michelle Obama issues. Beyoncé is classed among the Josephine Bakers, the Millie Jacksons, the Ma Raineys and Bessie Smiths. Her connection to these bawdy traditions of blues and soul are remixed in a contemporary R&B and Hip Hop package that frequently makes Black feminists lose their minds, some out of unparalleled pleasure, others out of unparalleled dismay.

Bey knows others objectify her body, and it seems she kind of likes it. In the "Partition" video for her 2013 visual and self-titled album *Beyoncé,* her actual, unretouched ass is a character in many of the video's scenes. This kind of self-objectification feels celebratory for some feminists and retrograde and dangerous to others.

Thus, there are risks to Michelle Obama's choice to align herself with Beyoncé socially. On the one hand, she gets cool points from younger crowds. On the other hand, many Black women might clutch their pearls at Michelle Obama's embrace of a Black woman who is frequently understood within the mythos of unbridled Black female sexuality. Whereas Beyoncé's unapologetic focus on her body and sex appeal frequently causes her to be perceived as a threat to children by soccer-mom types who wish she would simply cover up and stop gyrating, many moms love the idea of their children doing a more chaste form of gyration with Michelle Obama for her Let's Move! campaign.

During the launch of that campaign, Beyoncé remixed her 2006 song and video, "Get Me Bodied," a bass-driven club anthem, into the child and family-friendly "Move Your Body," a savvy marketing decision which helped make the campaign seem fun and exciting for children. In this regard, Michelle Obama's engagement with a pop icon created a context to make her campaign socially relevant and impactful.

But the First Lady has also chosen more risky allegiances with Beyoncé, particularly in her husband's final term. When Beyoncé performed with Coldplay at the 2016 Super Bowl, the Obamas sat down with Gayle King to discuss their Super Bowl–watching plans. Michelle told Gayle, "I care deeply about the Halftime Show. Deeply. I got dressed for the Halftime Show. I hope Beyoncé likes what I have on." The First Lady was dressed in a black blouse with black slacks. Several hours later, Beyoncé performed her new hit "Formation," a song whose video offered an overt critique of anti-Black state violence, while wearing an all-black leather outfit and a makeshift breastplate made of bullets. A salute to the fiftieth anniversary of the founding of the Black Panther Party, the clear celebration of the Black Power Movement unsettled many white Americans who claimed that Beyoncé and her dancers were anti-police.

But Mrs. Obama's coy overture in all Black to the impending performance offers perhaps a slight window into her love affair with Beyoncé. During the President's 2008 campaign, in an infamous cover called "The Politics of Fear," the *New Yorker* satirized an iconic campaign fist bump that Michelle gave Barack prior to one of his speeches, by ginning her up in a Black Power–era Afro, and slinging a machine gun around her body, with a strap across her chest made of bullets.

Eight years later, Beyoncé's Superbowl costume, a clear tribute to the sartorial choices of the Black Panther Party, perhaps unwittingly, invoked this image as well. It was backlash over the image coupled with hand-wringing and vitriol toward Mrs. Obama during the President's first campaign that caused her to retreat to the safer position of mom-in-chief. Eight years earlier, in February 2008, Michelle Obama said on the campaign trail, "For the first time in my adult lifetime, I'm really proud of my country," a remark that celebrated Barack's success in the primaries and America's ostensible desire to overcome its long history of racial discrimination. Before we knew Michelle Obama as mom-in-chief, we knew her as the well-educated, politically thoughtful, and appropriately critical wife of a young politician with a rising star.

Her unassuming honesty about the ways that racism had challenged her faith in American democracy also betrayed something of the political discontent that many sisters feel with the American political system. Her candor unfortunately situated her within the rhetorical realm of the Angry Black Woman, a shift that is a surefire way to discredit the legitimate claims Black women make about the limitations of American democracy.

In Beyoncé then Michelle Obama has

found someone who is not bound by the same expectations of respectability, or rhetorical reticence, or the performance of chaste sexuality that shapes the lives of public Black women. To the extent that people try to police and regulate Beyoncé's choices in this manner, she takes great pleasure in flouting the rules of social propriety.

Where Michelle Obama's fist bump and the subsequent satirizing of it fueled the racial panic of white Americans and might conceivably have cost her husband the presidency, Beyoncé could forthrightly invoke this history. Beyoncé's Super Bowl performance demanded some level of social reckoning with the truth of the Black Power Movement, and its descendant, the current Movement for Black Lives, in ways that Michelle Obama could never do. But Michelle's quip to Gayle that she hoped "Beyoncé likes what I have on" suggests not only some level of Black girl solidarity, but also the sense that the song "Formation" gave voice to matters that would otherwise go unvoiced for the First Lady.

More than two decades ago, Darlene Clark Hine, a historian of Black women at Northwestern University, wrote about the ways that race women had perfected a *cul-*

ture of dissemblance, a strategy of moving through social space in which Black women gave the appearance of openness, while holding their most private, innermost thoughts, desires and lives in abeyance from public consumption. Michelle Obama's path to dissemblance has been fraught with struggle. Her candor in the early days of her husband's campaign was a study in her failure to dissemble.

That time she was caught on camera rolling her eyes at John Boehner after he made a terrible joke is another example. While it is rare for any Black woman in the public eye not to hold her cards tight to her chest — Oprah is the exception — Michelle Obama has not seemed interested in gripping her cards as tightly as she has ultimately been forced to do.

In her love and admiration for Beyoncé, she tips her hand a bit. That relationship challenges a myriad of historical narratives that shape American public perception about Black women's lives. Excepting Oprah and Gayle, we have rarely been treated to seeing unabashed admiration between two sisters at the top of their game. The other exception would be the Williams sisters, but then, they are actual blood kin.

Black women know full well that our lives

are nothing without the sisters who inspire us, pull our cards, make us laugh uproariously, and show up for every manner of celebration or rescue mission, depending on what is required. We are our sisters' keepers. So at one level, Michelle and Beyoncé's relationship is not qualitatively different from any number of other powerful encounters Black women have, when we walk into a room, see that other sister winning, and catch the twinkle in her eye because the feeling — the *pride* — is mutual.

But we should not act like such Black women's friendships are forged on easy terrain. We have to travel through a landmine of shame, stereotypes, distrust, and pain to get to each other. We have to pull off the shades and stop the dissimulation for just a moment sometimes to see and reciprocate that twinkle in the eyes — that look of recognition.

Michelle Obama and Beyoncé Knowles-Carter don't travel across easy terrain to embrace one another. They travel through histories that would deny the visceral pleasure of sexiness to a First Lady like Michelle, and one that would deny the privileges of respectability to an otherwise traditional, privileged upper-middle-class Black girl like Beyoncé.

Both Michelle and Beyoncé are actively remixing the terms upon which Black womanhood has been cast. The denial of the right to ladyhood that has shaped Black women's lives since the advent of slavery can no longer proceed unchecked into the twenty-first century. For Michelle Obama has been a consummate lady, despite her haters' claims to the contrary. Like Bey said, "Y'all haters corny with that . . . mess."

The thing is, though: maybe it was never Michelle's goal to be the consummate Black lady. Maybe like many high-achieving Black girls, she wanted her ladyhood to be a strategy, a tool, a performance she could pull out of the briefcase when necessary, and store it away again when no longer required. On more than a few occasions, I'm sure the First Lady has wanted to tell some of her haters to bow down. For instance, her official White House portrait caused a minor controversy, when the First Lady opted for a sleeveless dress for the photo. Two years later, Representative Jim Sensenbrenner of Wisconsin remarked that Michelle Obama had a "big butt," and thus no business leading the Let's Move! campaign. Surely she wanted to tell his ass to bow down. Sometimes ratchet is a more appropriate register in which to check your haters than respectability will ever be. But overtly ratchet Mrs. Obama simply cannot be. Beyoncé can be as ratchet as she wants to be though, and in this, I think the First Lady finds a place to let her hair down and put her middle fingers up.

In those moments, I can imagine Michelle reading the words of her critics, and responding like Beyoncé might: "You know you that bitch when you cause all this conversation." Her husband has certainly followed Beyoncé's husband's lead in dealing with his haters, once famously "brushing that dirt off [his] shoulders," in a speech, like Jay-Z told us all to do in response to our haters. The Knowles-Carters routinely provide anthems that the Obamas can live by.

The U.S. is no nation for Black women. It is too limited a container for the magic we bring. And because the American national imaginary is built on the most limited and stingy ideas about who Black women get to be, when we are called to navigate the terrain of racial representation as public figures, many sisters return to the most basic truth we have — we need each other to survive. Michelle Obama needs Beyoncé. I say need, not in the way that you need a drink of water. But rather in the way that you need to be able to see and love yourself — not only in your own eyes but in the eyes of another sister. Every sister who spends a fair amount of time navigating predominantly white professional environments knows that you need some kind of anthem to help you decompress after you twerk, wine, and two-step your way through racial micro-aggressions, while making that shit look like you waltzed.

For many, many of us, our anthems of choice come from Bey. She is our friend in our head, that girl that says the stuff that you wish you could say, but can't.

In many ways, the friendship between Lady O and the King Bey is remarkable. But when you get right down to it, that kind of Black girl friendship is as regular as rain. Or maybe as regular as *reign* is more precise. When Black girls win, we all win. These two Black girls win on the regular, and long after they have departed their respective thrones, Black girls will win more easily because they were here — together.

WE GO WAY BACK

YLONDA GAULT CAVINESS

We go way back. Back to the enchanting little-Black-girl rhythms of wooden paddle balls, jacks and double Dutch ditties: "Ice cream, ice cream; cherry on top. How many boyfriends does 'Chelle got? 1-2-3-4 . . ."

We go back like well-greased afro puffs, boney knees and narrow hips — shaking till our backbones slip. Back like playing the dozens with Pumkin, June Bug and Tiny — whose pretty moon face and wide-bodied frame never let a honeybun go unloved. We shared secrets, dance moves, *Right On!* magazine centerfolds and grape Now & Laters.

It was the 1970s. She and I reveled in our Blackness, in our fineness — at the *same damn time.* Modest means did not define us, instead emboldened us, sharpened our senses — granting license to cast the "don't-come-for-me" stank-eye to any interloper out to test the bad-assery we wore with the ease and pride of bold-printed culottes.

Please! I been knowing Michelle La-Vaughn Robinson. Her power, her style, her stance, her cadence — every idiosyncrasy, including the single raised eyebrow and pursed lip half-smile — is as familiar to me as stove-top hot combs and fried chicken gizzards. If you don't know what I'm talking about, you better ask somebody.

Just don't ask 'Chelle. When she burst on to the national scene as Mrs. Barack Obama a decade ago, she and I needed no introduction. We are old friends.

My girl does not suffer foolishness. She will graciously oblige but, with a knowing look, I can tell that she is not here for simple-minded queries into her intrinsic strength, her mother wit, or her straight-up truth.

I saw it back in 2007, when *60 Minutes'* Steve Kroft asked if she feared for her husband's safety as a presidential candidate, Michelle Obama looked dead in the camera: "The reality is that as a Black man, Barack can get shot at the gas station."

Translation: "Please. We all know what time it is."

Months later, she gave me and other women an insider wink with CNN's Larry King. In an attempt to contrast the Bush administration's stubborn stance on warring with Iraq, King wanted to know if the then-presumptive presidential nominee had a mind that could be changed. "I change it every day," she deadpanned.

In other words: "You better recognize."

The white media establishment was not ready. *New York Times* columnist Maureen Dowd wrote: "She came on strong . . . I wince a bit when Michelle Obama chides . . . casting Barack as an undisciplined child."

Days later, when Mrs. Obama sat her tall, dark and lovely self down with *The View*'s round-tabled hosts, Barbara Walters wanted her reaction to the piece: "I can't even give that any attention . . ." Michelle said. "She [Dowd] doesn't know me . . . [or] what's going on in our household."

Paraphrase: "Girl, bye."

Mrs. Obama does not back down. No, she didn't stutter in February 2008 when we heard her say, "For the first time in my adult lifetime, I am really proud of my country." Clarifying the statement on *The View*, she countered that "only in America" could working-class parents on the South Side of Chicago send her and her brother to Princeton University. But until primary voters turned out in such large numbers, she was not certain "we, as a nation," could look past race.

In other words: "I ain't sorry."

Why should she be apologetic? Come to think of it, why should I? Michelle did not come to play. Yes, she is proud in her role as Mrs. Obama and, rightly so, she gives Barack his propers all day long, loving and supporting his candidacy. But she never set out to function as a mere prop to his — or anyone else's — agenda. Fearlessly and fiercely, everything about this startling "bad-mama-jamma" from the Chi shouted to the world: I am a strong Black woman. And not strong in that long-suffering, carrying-the-burdens-of-generations way many of us have come to know from our mamas, their mamas and the mamas before them. Strong in a brand-new way. A strong that declares, "You don't get to define me. Only *I* get to define me."

It may seem like a reach; certainly my intention is not to disrespect our ancestors in any way. But Michelle Obama set me free!

Probably, she set all women free, in a way. Sojourner Truth once said: "If women want rights more than they got, why don't they just take them and not be talking about it?"

Two Black First Ladies Walk into a Room

CHIRLANE MCCRAY

We were backstage in a hotel event space in Manhattan. It was just moments before she had to go out and speak to supporters. I could hear the bustle of setting up on the other side of the heavy velvet curtain and the click of heels as people moved across the wooden floor. The lights were dim and I still remember the chairs they rounded up so we could sit together in the barren backstage area. They were straight-backed and uncomfortable. It was a short while after Bill was sworn in as mayor. And I had asked to see First Lady Michelle Obama while she was in town; I knew exactly what I wanted to ask her, but I was a little nervous.

Some people might think two Black First Ladies would have a whole lot to talk about. And we probably did. After all we were both working mothers of color devoted to our families. And we both had ambitious partners in public office. I was the newbie First Lady in New York City. She was six years settled in as First Lady of the USA on a grand, national stage. But we were also in different stages of life. She was my junior, a hair short of a decade, with two young children. I had one child in college and was soon to be an empty nester.

Also understand that everything changes once you become a public person. A person on whom some folks pin their hopes and dreams. A person under constant scrutiny. A person often under fire for, well, just about everything. Too Black. Not Black enough. Too feminist. Not feminist enough. Too political. Not political enough. And to be a Black woman is to know there are many people you will not please — just for being alive.

There are suddenly many, many, many new people in your personal space. Some are phenomenally helpful. Some are not. New relationships take time.

And time is very, very precious.

So here we are, two Black First Ladies, meeting solo for the very first time, with only minutes to spare. I thanked her for her service to our country, thanked her for the kindness of taking time to speak with me. And I'm saying this, while still standing and looking up in awe at a whole lot of tall and gorgeous. After all, this was Michelle Obama, a woman navigating an extremely challenging position of power with exceptional grace, confidence and poise (who also happens to have a lot of inches on me).

At first we made some small talk about our kids, just like I'd done with other moms on countless park benches. Finally I asked her: Do you have any advice for me?

If you care enough about Michelle Obama to be reading this, it probably won't surprise you to learn that she did not offer me a clichéd response about following my passions. With a sternness that is refreshing in retrospect but was quite a bit to absorb at the time, she talked about the kind of practical support and staffing I would need, including a chief of staff, scheduler and communications director. Surround yourself with people you trust, she told me. And she stressed how I would have to protect my personal time.

I listened carefully, almost wishing I had a recorder. And then, as she was standing up to leave, her tone softened and she said with assurance, "You'll be alright." I smiled. She smiled. And then she put her game face on and went out to meet the people.

I often think back on that conversation,

and whenever I do the soundness of her advice becomes increasingly clear. But I have learned even more from the First Lady by observing her from afar. The way she has arranged her life reveals a lot about who she is and what she cares about. And the way her life is portrayed and perceived has much to teach us about what it means to be a woman in the twenty-first century.

When First Lady Obama said her top priority was to serve as mom-in-chief, she was telling us that her family comes first. It must have been a huge challenge to be uprooted from her home, find new schools for her girls, get them acclimated to a new life, and also take on a new role and new responsibilities while being a supportive, loving spouse. I have tremendous respect for how she defined herself, right from the beginning, defined her role before there was too much speculation about what she would do. And she brought her mother, someone she could trust without reservation, to live with them in the White House. Such a smart move! And, by all accounts, Malia and Sasha are growing up to be as poised as their famous parents.

I am relieved that we do not see them in the media that often, but when I do I get a kick out of how regular they appear. It is no small trick to raise children and have a healthy marriage while living in the spotlight. It's one thing to have a tired child meltdown on the playground. Imagine that happening around hundreds of people with cell phone cameras! I count my blessings that our children, Chiara and Dante, were older before Bill became mayor, able to get through most of their teen years without the intense scrutiny that comes with public office. As we reflect on the Obama presidency, we must not limit our gratitude to Barack and Michelle alone — their entire family has made enormous sacrifices for our country and won the respect of the world.

While I have no doubt that her amazing, loving family is the First Lady's proudest achievement, her work obviously extends well beyond the domestic sphere. Although no First Lady receives a salary, the title comes with traditions and countless expectations. Of course, it also comes with enormous opportunities to do good. To be First Lady of the United States is to be stuck between a rock — what the world expects of you — and a hard place — what you expect from yourself. The only way forward is to tread carefully and have faith in your own sense of direction.

The First Lady has done exactly that with

Let's Move!, her signature initiative to solve the challenge of childhood obesity within one generation. For starters, Let's Move! is as big and ambitious as many of the President's efforts, which shows that she is not afraid to embrace the full potential of her platform and tackle one of the most urgent public health crises facing our nation. Right now, nearly one in three children in this country is overweight or obese, and the statistics are even more unacceptable in the African American and Hispanic communities. No one can argue with the urgency of this issue.

But I also love that she chose an initiative that nurtures her *own* physical and mental health, because if you're not careful, being a First Lady can really mess with you. I can testify! With all those event meals, it's tough to keep track of all the calories you're eating. And if you're sitting in meetings, you are sitting — that is, you are not exercising. With Let's Move!, the First Lady stayed well by doing good. And when you see her at a Let's Move! event, harvesting vegetables or playing flag football, it always looks like she's having *fun,* which doesn't surprise me a bit. One of the best things about my job is having opportunities to read, play and make art with young New Yorkers. If helping our young people is a stereotypical First Lady thing to do, then that is one stereotype I am happy to perpetuate.

Let's Move! also allows the First Lady to get out into the world and interact with folks outside the Beltway bubble. That is not a small thing. Think about it. It's not really home if you can't throw open a window for a breath of fresh air or take a walk alone or run to the store to grab some peanut butter by yourself. And virtually every word you say, any position on any subject, must first be filtered through a team of communication specialists.

Serving as First Lady on any stage comes with enormous privileges. But in order to truly appreciate and honor everything First Lady Obama has achieved, we must first understand that all First Ladies — like most women — are still trapped in a box of outdated expectations.

In First Lady Obama's case, it is a fabulous white box on a very large stage, and she has done a lot to push the walls back and expand our understanding of what a political marriage can be. But the walls are still there, and they are still terribly restrictive.

As I write this, the First Lady's approval rating is remarkably high, given this era of scorched-earth media coverage. But while I think she deserves every percentage point and more, I wonder: To what degree is her popularity a function of how divine she looks in a dress? And how many of us envy her toned arms as much as her intellect? Just like every woman, she is still judged first and foremost by her appearance, and where she falls on a scale of "fierce" to "frumpy."

Because we are pummeled with air-brushed, magazine-cover versions of Michelle Obama, it's easy to forget who she was before becoming became First Lady. The brilliant Harvard Law student who marched in the streets to push her school to hire minority professors doesn't get talked about, and have we forgotten the highly capable executive who worked as Vice President for Community and External Affairs at the University of Chicago? How does Michelle's past connect to the Michelle Obama who became First Lady? Are her poll numbers a reflection of her impressive history and attributes?

Every political spouse, myself included, must weigh how her words and actions will reflect on her partner. The First Lady learned early on that opponents of her husband would not hesitate to twist her words to suit their purposes. I'm thinking about that time back in 2008, when they tried to paint her as Benedict Arnold after she said "For the first time in my adult lifetime, I am really proud of my country because it feels like hope is finally making a comeback." The meaning of her statement was twisted when it was shortened to, "For the first time in my adult life, I am really proud of my country." When you go through nonsense like that, it's only natural to become cautious.

And of course there are different rules for Black women — the judgments come more quickly, and they are far more difficult to overturn. Doesn't it make a lot of sense for a no-nonsense kind of woman like Michelle to survive this madness by moving through the world with "show, don't tell" and "if you can't be free, be a mystery" determination?

But I still feel a little cheated. Have we made *any* progress over the years? Will our next First Lady have an easier time of it, or will the box Michelle Obama so valiantly expanded shrink back to its previous dimensions?

America's reaction to the passing of First Lady Nancy Reagan is a fascinating case study of how far we have come — and how far we still have to go.

I was stunned by the tone of her obituaries and remembrances. Sure, there was the typical pablum about her fabulous frocks (the *New York Post:* "Behold, Nancy Reagan's 10 greatest outfits"), but all of a sudden the press couldn't contain their praise for her strength, her influence, her unbreakable partnership with President Reagan — qualities that were held against her as First Lady. In fact, when she was in the White House some three decades ago, critics labeled her a "dragon lady" and implied that she should be seen and not heard. Every move she made was viewed with suspicion, and many Americans seemed to think she abdicated her right to be a free-thinking woman of action when her husband became president.

Apparently Nancy Reagan thought otherwise. She considered it her right to speak her mind and offer advice whenever it might be helpful to him. After all, the oath of office does not override the vows of marriage.

Now that she's gone, America seems to agree with First Lady Reagan. But no such luxury has been afforded to her successors; the specter of being smeared as a "dragon lady" or worse — *much* worse — has not gone away. First Lady Barbara Bush was labeled "America's grandmother" and is largely perceived as a traditional First Lady, although it only takes a few clicks to find articles that question whether she had an undue influence over her husband (or her sons). First Lady Laura Bush was often portrayed as someone whose passion was books, not public life, which is surely a gross oversimplification. And of course, Secretary Hillary Clinton's experience as First Lady is proof of how vehemently some will fight the idea of our president taking full advantage of his partner's skills and knowledge. If Secretary Clinton returns to the White House in January, it will be fascinating to see how First Gentleman Bill Clinton is covered by the press. My guess is that we won't see many slideshows documenting his ten greatest outfits.

As a society, it is long past time for us to move beyond these "isms" and realize that we all benefit when our elected leaders are blessed with equally strong partners. We need to start celebrating female achievement in real time, not after the fact. And let's start with Michelle Obama. We don't hear much these days about her influence behind the scenes. But as I recall that backstage conversation we shared and the assured look on her face as she dropped her hard-earned knowledge on me, I am certain that we haven't yet begun to understand the crucial role she played as partner to her husband.

I hope we will, one day soon. I am delighted that the First Lady has launched her global initiative, Let Girls Learn. And she has said that she plans to do some writing too. I, for one, have my fingers crossed for a memoir that charts her remarkable journey.

Perhaps one day we will sit together over a cup of hot tea or glass of wine and chat about the road ahead and the paths we have carved out for ourselves.

My prayer is that this book is just the beginning of a celebration that will only become louder and more jubilant, as Michelle Obama's legacy grows alongside our gratitude for her giving so generously of herself.

Becoming the

CATHI HANAUER

The truth is, I don't know much abou
chelle Obama, other than what everyone
knows. She's tall, she's radiant, and yeah,
the woman rocks some beautiful clothes.
Her smile is both drop-dead and genuine.
She can dance, and she's brilliant. And her
arms? I can't even.

In fact, as a tiny, scrawny white woman
who couldn't dance if the floor was on fire,
wouldn't know a Jason Wu dress from a
Target bargain frock, and spends most of
her work day in bed under fourteen blankets
(I'm a writer, I live in New England, we
keep the heat low), I wouldn't be surprised
if someone suggested I'm about as unlike
Michelle Obama as two women roughly the
same age with two children can be. Yet, in
one way — and it's an important one — I
really identify with Michelle. And that's this:
She and I have both had to learn to be The
Wife.

like this. When I met my
was a 27-year-old magazine
York, working for a well-
nly in a job that had both
u perks. I had landed an intern-
the summer before senior year of
they'd hired me back on gradua-
tion, and I'd worked my way up to senior
editor by age 25 — not so unlike Michelle
(other than, okay, our salaries, educations,
credentials . . .), who by 25 was already a
successful corporate lawyer in Chicago. My
job was fun, challenging, exhilarating. But
— like Michelle — I wanted something that
felt, to me, a little more meaningful. She
wanted, it's now known, to get out of
corporate law and do something that would
allow her to "give back" and "exhort others
to do the same." I wanted to write novels.

And so, after a few years of taking fiction
workshops at night and spending weekends
scribbling away, I applied to MFA pro-
grams. I picked one that was both affordable and a nice life-change (Hello, University of Arizona), traded my full-time job for
a monthly advice column, at the same
magazine, that would mostly fund my new
lower-cost life . . . and off I went to spend a

blissful two years in the desert immersed in reading and writing.

That's where I met Dan.

To be accurate, we met when I flew out to visit the school and asked the director for names of some women in the program I might talk to. Dan was not a woman (nor is he now), but somehow his name made the list, and all the women were too busy while he was happy to grab a free lunch.

Michelle met Barack when, as a 25-year-old associate at the Sidley & Austin Chicago law firm, she was asked to mentor a summer associate named Barack Obama, a 27-year-old Harvard Law School prodigy who was described by one of his professors as possibly the most gifted student she'd ever taught. Michelle, no sucker for superlatives (she herself was once called, by a partner at S&A, "possibly the most ambitious associate that I've ever seen"), was instantly suspicious. *What's with that name?* she's reputed to have thought. And was she really being asked to mentor this dude just because they were both Black in a mostly White firm? Justifiably, she approached the whole thing with a hint of wariness. As she told David Mendell, the author of *Obama: From Promise to Power,* "I figured he was one of these smooth brothers who could talk straight and impress people." Still, she took him to lunch, despite his "bad sport jacket and a cigarette dangling from his mouth."

I, too, had been suspicious when I met Dan. Why was this person available for lunch when so many women weren't? At the time — in year four of the three-year program — he was teaching a class or two and working on his writing until he figured out what was next. Smart, calm, and contemplative, Dan was a nice contrast to my control-freak, first-born, Type A mania. (In fact, as the second-born of two and a reliable Type B, he was held back in kindergarten because he barely talked before age five; his older brother did the talking for him.) Over sandwiches, I peppered him with questions that were as much about him as about the graduate program.

After college, he'd moved to Park City, Utah, where he worked as a ski instructor (winters) and a janitor (all seasons) for a few years until mopping floors got old and he applied to graduate school and ambled down to Tucson. At the time we met, he was earning about an eighth of what I was, living in a small room in a house with two women (i.e., someone else could be counted on to replace the toilet paper and wipe the

106

counters), and driving a 12-year-old Subaru with nonworking A/C (this was the desert, remember) and 175,000 miles on it.

Similarly, Barack's car, when he met Michelle, "had so much rust on it that there was a rusted hole in the passenger door," she told her local newspaper, the *Hyde Park Herald.* He was broke, his wardrobe was "cruddy," and he "wasn't ever going to try to impress me with things." And yet, somehow he charmed her. After their initial lunch, he took her to a community organizing meeting, and she saw the way he connected with people (getting a hint of the big dreams he had — and that he might actually accomplish some of them). He was "the real deal," she said. Soon they were dating, and now, rather than being put off by his differences — his white Kansas grandmother, that he was raised "on an island" (Hawaii) — she was intrigued.

Around the same time, 1,700 miles southwest of there, Dan was, for his part, charming *me.* He wore faded jeans, faded shirts, big (faded) work boots, sunglasses that, when not on his eyes, dangled from a stretchy thing around his neck. (I wore, as he tells it, black Ray Bans that covered most of my face and an enormous black leather coat in the oven-like heat.)

Still, I wouldn't fall for Dan — or believe he was quite the star he was reputed to be in the program — until I saw his supposedly brilliant stories for myself. So I requested some writing samples from his classes, including, if he dared, his own. And before I knew it, I was sitting in a bubble bath reading one of his stories, and going, "Whoa. This guy can write."

One thing led to another, for us and for Michelle and Barack, and one day — in fact, less than three months apart the exact same year — 1992 — all four of us married: Dan and me, Barack and Michelle. She changed her name; I didn't; she wore a much more traditional wedding dress (mine was tea length, strapless, and, okay, a little slutty). And then all four of us continued to pursue our work. In Dan's and my case, we maintained separate residences at first, since I didn't want a husband distracting me from the novel I was writing. Michelle, it's been said, felt similarly about her career: "Barack and I have lived very separate professional lives," she said of their pre-POTUS/FLOTUS years. "He's done his thing, I do my thing."[1]

Dan eventually finished the writing program, with enough published stories to comprise a collection. But he didn't have luck publishing the book as a whole — which might have led to a teaching job somewhere — so we moved back to New York, and he got a job as an assistant program editor at *Stagebill* magazine, making $18K a year. Then — praise the lord — I sold my novel in a two-book deal.

We lived in a one-bedroom walkup in a mouse-friendly tenement above a bakery, where the power went out weekly, the couple upstairs fought so violently we once had to call the cops, and, at times, brown water ran mysteriously down our bathroom walls. But we were surviving, sort of, and pursuing our dreams, more or less.

And then I got pregnant. The baby was planned and wanted; we were both 31, ready to attempt a family. But the triple whammy, for me, of nonstop "morning" sickness plus trying to learn how the hell one takes care of a child; a second novel under contract that was proving much harder to write than the first; and the loss of the devoted and insightful community of writers an MFA program can provide — all along with the expense of living in New York — took its toll. And that's when — like Michelle! — I first realized that motherhood was not something I could do on the side while fulfilling my work ambitions. The next decade for both of us was a nonstop flurry of work, marriage, running a household, and birthing, nursing, and raising two young children. Of it, Michelle — who eventually left corporate law first to work for the mayor, then to direct a program that provided leadership training and mentoring for young people, and then, by the time her older daughter was seven, to be a VP at the University of Chicago Hospitals — has said: "I wake up every morning wondering how on the earth I am going to pull off that next minor miracle of getting through the day."[2]

My own similar struggles took the form of creating and editing an essay anthology called *The Bitch in the House,* which, when published in 2002, became a bestseller. The book was about realizing, once we walked through the doors feminism had opened for my generation and Michelle's, that at the end of the day, you still were The Mother, The Homemaker, The Wife — all in a manner your husband wasn't. Put another way: Unless you were one of those rare women who could relinquish the role of Primary Parent *and* were married to one of those rare men who could and would take it on, your priority had to be the children and running the household. It's been said that

Barack is a loving, compassionate father, and I'm sure that's the truth; after all, why wouldn't his naturally warm personality carry down to the way he raises his kids? But it's also been said that Michelle, gorgeous as she is in designer dresses, still wears the pants in that family when it comes to the *family,* and I'm sure that's the truth, too. Someone, after all, has to buy the kids' clothing, set up the parent-teacher conferences, and know when the daughters' basketball games are (not to mention bring the sliced oranges on Snack Day and get *both* parents to show up now and then) — even in the White House. And it's hard to imagine that someone being the same man who, as a U.S. Senator in 2004 — and just as Michelle was asking herself those hard questions about work-life balance — was, as described in the *Washington Post,* "dazzling the country with his eloquence at the 2004 Democratic National Convention and being talked about as a presidential candidate";[3] even harder to imagine that same someone being the man who was responsible for both the death of Osama bin Laden and the passing of health care reform in America.

Thus, for the Obamas, that person was, and still is, Michelle. Not so much when she married Barack, but when she became a mother, and then when she agreed, albeit reluctantly, first to take leave from her lucrative job to campaign for Barack, and eventually to move her daughters and her own mother from Chicago to D.C. so her husband could become president. In all of those ways, Michelle, arguably as brilliant, talented, and capable as her husband, gave up at least some of the carefully constructed and nurtured career path she saw for herself in order to be President Barack Obama's faithful wife and FLOTUS.

This is not, mind you, to say that Michelle quit working when her luggage showed up in D.C. The woman is not sitting around eating presidential bon bons at 1600 Pennsylvania Avenue, though I certainly hope the perks of her job allow her a few now and then. But what did change, work-wise, for Michelle — as it did for me, and as it does for so many college-educated women, particularly once children are involved — is that we both reached a point in our lives and marriages when we agreed to become the "helpmate" — The Wife — as our husbands took on the more important and lucrative work role. We did this for the greater good of our marriages, our families, and in Michelle's case, the world; and maybe even, as mothers, for ourselves. Michelle became Mrs. President. And I became Mrs. *Modern Love.*

This, for me, happened after I published *The Bitch in the House,* and then Dan followed with *The Bastard on the Couch* (subtitled *27 Men Try Really Hard to Explain Their Feelings about Love, Loss, Fatherhood, and Freedom).* Cute, right? *The New York Times* thought so. They asked us to bring that kind of material to their pages by starting an as-yet-unnamed personal essay column about relationships.

By then, we'd left New York and were living a more affordable, child-centered life in a small town in Massachusetts. I was collecting *Bitch* royalties, writing my novel and occasional magazine pieces, raising the kids, and feeling happier and less overwhelmed than I'd felt in years. Dan, less happily, was underemployed as a consultant for his former full-time New York employer, so he was thrilled about the *Times* possibility. I — like Michelle when Barack first suggested he might get into politics, and then later when he wanted to run for president — was not. I liked working independently, and I couldn't, at least for myself, fathom a hard weekly deadline. At that point, we didn't have a regular babysitter and lived far from

113

family. Our kids attended school at a small public co-op where the parents were required to help out. I put the meals in our fridge and on our table; I — like Michelle, I'm sure — managed the family calendar, the carpools, the sports teams, illnesses and doctors, houseguests and birthday parties. Dan, for his part, did the cars, lawn, bills, home repairs, and technology. He taught the kids Scrabble (and poker), took them to Friendly's for dinner when I needed time. It worked, for me. I was making a living doing what I wanted, with, finally, the flexibility and headspace to also be the mother I needed to be. I didn't want to mess with that.

But I also couldn't exactly say no to the *Times* offer when Dan wanted it, could I?

So I agreed I would help him launch the column, and then we'd see if he could take it over. Maybe that was just the teensiest bit like Michelle agreeing to help Barack run for president, though in her case knowing that, if he won, it would change her career, her life, and the lives of their family irreparably. But eventually, and happily for us, she came around. "Politics might be a more noble pursuit than she originally believed," wrote Myra G. Gutin in *The Washington Post*. Moreover, "running for president was something Barack needed to do or else forever wonder what might have been."

It all worked. Barack became our president and Dan became Mr. *Modern Love,* each man successful at his task while his wife did her part — minor in my case, major in Michelle's — and also held down the home front. I don't need to list President Obama's myriad accomplishments in his eight years on the job. As for Dan's, now in his twelfth year of editing *Modern Love,* he's turned it into one of the most popular features in the Sunday *New York Times.* The column has spawned a TV pilot, a full-length musical, a CD, fifty books, and a podcast that recently launched as Number One on iTunes. He's no POTUS, I'm no FLOTUS, our kids are no KOPOTUSes (figure it out). But we are not displeased with — or untickled by — the success of that column, just as, I'm sure, Michelle is not displeased by her husband's run in the White House, and maybe even, just a little, by the power and respect that his position has brought her.

Still, for her, that respect was neither easy nor immediate. I can't imagine that, proud as she was of her husband and the work he was doing, there weren't some moments of ambivalence about his sudden rise to Leader of the Free World while she, a formerly tough-ass lawyer, was now relegated to *First Lady* and *mom-in-chief* — even if she's the one who coined the latter phrase; even if, by that point, she herself said she would, on top of everything else she was handling, only "work" two and a half days a week. Michelle now lived on a stage, and there's no question she needed to get used to that. Anyone would.

Yet she did it. She amped up her marital and political commitment, learned to be herself without offending the press and the haters, and even seemed to suddenly be having fun in the role — whether swishing for the White House dunk cam, dancing on *Ellen,* or having Beyoncé play at her birthday bash. What's more, whatever resentment she still had toward her husband (and let's face it, we all have *some* now and then) seemed to morph into a combination of affection and even amusement at his degree of royalty. I picture her watching him, her eyebrows raised as he tries to explain or extricate from something and millions of people hang on his every word, and thinking, *Dude, you* know *you just phoned that one in.* To her, he was the same old Barack: sweet, smart, adorable, but leaving his socks by the bed and forgetting to put away the damn butter.

As for me, happy as I was about the success of the *Modern Love* column, it took some getting used to the fact that, outside of our family, my husband was suddenly and definitely just plain more important than me; that I was now, partly by my own choosing, officially the primary parent and runner of the house. Certainly this was not what I'd anticipated when we'd met, married, and decided to start a family. Everything in my life — from my education to my early jobs to my post-feminist ideas — had led me to believe that my husband and I could work, earn, and parent equally. I simply hadn't realized how complicated and exhausting and, for me, anger-inducing that would prove to be; that, when I found myself actually *in* that life — two jobs, two young kids, a bountiful but hamster-wheel life — I'd realize I wanted something a little less exhausting, and overwhelming, and unfair-seeming.

So becoming The Wife was in many ways a blessing and an opportunity for me — I was privileged to be able to cut back a little on my work, which most parents cannot afford to do — but it also, as with Michelle, took a little adjusting. I remember the moment, just a few years ago, when this . . . demotion? delegation? became most apparent to me. I had published two more books by then — Dan had too — and between books I was doing some editing and low-level writing. I still got the occasional fan letter or invitation to speak at a book club or class, though not compared to my *Bitch* days, and now, also, not compared to Dan. To be honest, I didn't mind. I was happy to stay home in pajamas working when I wasn't walking the dogs, taking a kid for new sneakers, overseeing a school schedule or college visit, grocery shopping, fighting for something important in my town, or even, one year, being the high school soccer booster club president (don't ask). I had time, now and then, to get a good night's sleep, read a novel, and enjoy my last few years with my children. I had started a fifth book: *The Bitch Is Back,* a sequel to the anthology that had spawned all this. But this time, the book was less about anger and more about making choices, in midlife, to find contentment.

Dan, in contrast, was traveling, teaching, speaking, appearing on radio and TV. Everywhere he went, he was swarmed with *Modern Love* lovers and people who wanted him to publish their essays. On tour for his fourth book, he filled performance spaces from L.A. to D.C. Women flirted and slipped him their manuscripts; men sidled up to make guy talk before mentioning a *Modern Love* idea they had.

Around that time, we attended a books festival at the University of Arizona — the same place, remember, where I'd once been a cool (if ridiculous) editor in Ray Bans. But now, *Dan* was the one not only invited to this event but asked to be a featured speaker. He was flown in and put up in a glitzy resort. And though I'd published the same number of books, I was merely "allowed" to come along, as Dan's wife.

At the opening reception he was a keynote speaker for a room of some 400. His speech was the usual hit; Dan is funny, compassionate, and wry. After the party, as we all milled around, another speaker — a nationally syndicated advice columnist, female and around my age — approached us. She was someone I would have bonded with a decade before; after all, I too had written a national and syndicated advice column, for seven years. I smiled, anticipating maybe chatting a little about editors, about hard questions we'd answered. But she looked past me, walked by, and reached for Dan's hand.

I felt my face go red, my blood pressure rise. But later, when I thought about it, I didn't blame her. There's a sad dichotomy in this country between working women and stay-at-home mothers and wives — something I was well aware of because I had *written books about it*! I knew this woman figured I'd have nothing of interest to say, in my presumed life of bake sales and midday Pilates classes. But I also knew that, in many ways, I had chosen this road I was on.

I suppose I've reached the point in the piece where I'm supposed to say, "And Michelle probably feels just like this too!" But now that I'm here, I can only say: Who am I kidding? Michelle is, yes, the POTUS's faithful wife, but her style and brilliance, her chutzpah and humor, her hard work and bright smile have made her a stellar presence in her own right. Michelle is Michelle. And I can't wait to see what she does next. And what she does after that, when her children are grown and she can focus with far fewer distractions on her career. She has said she'll never run for president herself. To that, I say: Never say never, Michelle. Let's just see where we all are a decade from now.

ON BEING FLAWLESSLY IMPERFECT

TIFFANY DUFU

It's only in recent decades that first ladies have been allowed to be imperfect. Until women like Eleanor Roosevelt, who on more than one occasion publicly disagreed with her husband's policies, and Betty Ford, who was transparent about her battle with alcoholism, the First Lady represented the embodiment of feminine perfection: Stepford Wife-in-Chief. Michelle Obama is only the third to have a professional or graduate degree, public evidence of intellectual prowess and independence, and to have balanced her own high-profile career with her private role as wife and mother. She, along with Hillary Clinton, charted a path that allows future first ladies to do it *their* way. Her polarity inspires all of us to break the mold.

Michelle Obama is a wife, mother, sister, daughter and friend. She is a career woman, civic volunteer, gardener, rapper, dancer, pet owner and fitness ambassador. She is funny, honest, and down to earth. She has managed to pull off a nearly impossible feminine feat: she is both liked and respected. And she accomplishes all of this on a global stage. Managing the details of her life must be exhausting, but she makes it look so *easy.*

How does she have it all?

The irony is that Michelle Obama makes it look easy precisely because she is complicated. Simultaneously flawless and imperfect, she brilliantly navigates opposing forces. And in the tension we can all see ourselves.

In my work, I address the daunting pressure women face to do it all. A woman's failure to do so is such a ubiquitous trope it has made for blockbuster comedy in films such as *I Don't Know How She Does It.* I've navigated this pressure myself and have learned that behind every great woman who isn't driving herself crazy to be perfect, there's a village of people who applaud and support her beautiful imperfections.

In Amy Cuddy's book, *Presence,* she defines presence as a "state of being attuned to and able to comfortably express our true thoughts, feelings, values and potential."[1] Michelle Obama has presence with a capital P in large part because she is comfortable with herself. The seeds of Mrs. Obama's self-assuredness were planted on the South Side of Chicago where her parents, Fraser and Marian Robinson, instilled in her enormous confidence. Her brother, Craig, remembers their father saying: "You don't want to do things because you're worried about people thinking they're right; you want to do the right things." According to Craig, being raised in this kind of environment: "You grow up not worrying about what people think about you."[2] The affirmation Michelle absorbed in her youth became the core of her current conviction about her identity. "I have never felt more confident in myself, more clear on who I am as a woman," she said a few months before she turned 50.[3]

I know from listening to hundreds of women's stories that powerful presence is only attained through recognizing our unique value. Yet even for me, understanding my value has been a tough journey. I remember sitting in a graduate school literary theory class, questioning my own credibility and feeling "lucky" that I was admitted into the program because deep down I didn't feel deserving. Twenty years later, in any room I'm in, whether I'm on a stage, in a parent-teacher conference, or sitting at a board table, I try to be cognizant of the lens that would be missing if my voice was absent. I've even taught myself how to recognize my value in a dressing room. I used to try on a dress, look in the mirror, and ask, "Can I wear this dress?" Now I pose confidently in the mirror and ask myself, "Can this dress wear *me*?" It's this feeling, that you are no longer a planet orbiting someone else's sun, but are now your own center of gravity, that Michelle emits so powerfully.

Michelle Obama isn't worried about what people think about her because she knows what she stands for. She puts herself out there to achieve her goal in ways the public has never seen a First Lady do. To build intimacy and goodwill she hugs everyone — including the Queen of England, who apparently hadn't been hugged in 57 years. To promote healthy eating she personally planted a garden on the White House lawn, which resulted in numerous press photos of her literally getting her hands dirty. For the first time in our nation's history we saw a sweaty First Lady. We've also seen one that raps and dances. In an effort to raise awareness about the importance of getting a college education, Michelle Obama teamed up with comedian Jay Pharoah to drop rhymes in a music video. To advocate healthy living and combat obesity, she challenged Ellen DeGeneres to an on-air dance-off. In her antics we see her vulnerability and her courage. Michelle Obama has beautifully established trust with millions of people, especially the nation's youth. "Although I'm the first lady of the United States, I'm no different from you," she told a group of high school students.[4] And we all believe her.

Michelle Obama has convinced us that she's "real" even though she lives in an alternate reality from the rest of us. Though it's likely been a long time since she stayed up all night making lemon bars for the school bake sale or had to feed her kids fast food from the drive-through at the end of a long working mommy day, when asked whether she's ever had a mom crisis she unequivocally responds, yes. "There's not a minute that goes by that I'm not hoping and praying that I'm doing right by these girls . . . All we can do is do our best . . . You don't know until it's over."

As a parent myself, on most days I doubt whether my job will ever be "over." It seems that with each developmental phase, what my kids require from me changes. Yet I remain consistent in my overall parenting strategy: focus eighty percent of your effort on being the kind of person you'd want your children to be. They are watching us carefully and they are sophisticated sponges. What I most want them to soak up is that they, too, can keep it real, that they can be the most authentic versions of themselves.

Michelle Obama is also both disciplined and flexible. For someone who makes it all look so natural, Michelle Obama is very well rehearsed. She likes control and puts herself in positions where the risk of a mistake or a surprise is minimal.[5] On the campaign trail she often spent hours researching and preparing for a speech. Just like her confidence, Michelle's work ethic was instilled early. Her father was the epitome of grit. His multiple sclerosis entitled him to disability benefits, yet he worked managing high-pressure water boilers at a water filtration plant his entire adult life, never retiring. Having a parent with a disability meant that Michelle learned the value of structure and the power of daily habits. As a student she would often stay up very late or get up early to study. Now that she's raising her own daughters, she is instilling in them a similar discipline. Though the Obamas are privileged with a staff to manage every household detail, Michelle insists that her daughters make their own beds each morning. She also picks one of their sports herself — to ensure the girls get regular practice doing something they don't necessarily like. Michelle Obama's number one rule? No whining.

In Rory Vaden's book, *Take the Stairs,* he explores the role that self-discipline plays in our success. In a world that values one-stop shopping and quick and easy recipes, it turns out that achieving what we want requires instituting mundane daily practice that we might not necessarily enjoy. For me, one of those practices is running. One mile can be grueling, especially on a cold, dark winter morning. Yet my physical fitness promotes endurance in other areas of my life, and I've never had so many aha moments or innovative ideas as when my body is in motion. I've met women whose self-discipline manifests in other ways. One of my colleagues sets her intention each morning at 5 a.m. through meditation. I recently met a young writer. She drafts ten pages per day with or without muse.

For the First Lady discipline is the key to excellence and exercising your highest potential. It's also the key to championship. When initially exploring a presidential bid with political consultants, including David Axelrod, it was Michelle who insisted they develop a strategy that would be the safest path to the White House. She wasn't interested in pursuing Barack's candidacy unless that was the number one goal. Michelle's mother, Marian, competed in the Illinois Senior Olympics right before turning sixty. "You don't just run to be running," she famously said, "you run to win."[6]

Michelle's commitment to discipline surprisingly gives way to flexibility. For her, achieving excellence requires adaptation. Michelle was furious on the campaign trail when campaign staffers were slow to give her feedback about her communication style, which was perceived in the media as too edgy. She wanted to be an asset to the campaign and insisted that she could adapt, which she did.[7] Fast forward eight years; her speech at the 2016 Democratic convention turned the tide of party divisiveness, inspired the nation, and was heralded as one of the best speeches in political convention history. Talk about taking the edge off.

One of the beautiful ways in which her flexibility manifests is in her willingness to meet people where they are, especially when they have opposing views. In 2001, Michelle had only been on her new job as director of community outreach for the University of Chicago medical center for a few weeks when an activist, Omar Shareef, disrupted the groundbreaking ceremony of a new children's hospital. He was leading protesters who accused the university of not giving enough business to African American construction workers. Michelle immediately invited Shareef to discuss the matter. She was savvy enough to know that the most effective way to represent the interest of the university was to meaningfully engage the local community and listen to their concerns. Within four weeks, she had brokered an agreement.[8]

Another way that Michelle reaches people where they are is by plugging into popular culture. Michelle Obama has mastered the art of leveraging celebrities that we care about to make us care about the things she does. She enlisted music heavy hitters Missy Elliott, Kelly Rowland, Janelle Monae, Jada Grace and Kelly Clarkson to release a song "This Is for My Girls." The hit single is the latest fuel for her Let Girls Learn/ #62MillionGirls initiative, which promotes girls' education globally. Michelle Obama's flexibility usually serves the cause. "There are many people who can't hear me precisely because I'm first lady of the United States," she recently told an audience at the interactive media festival South by Southwest.[9] She always has a message, but understands that she is not always the best person to deliver it.

Like her discipline, Michelle Obama is passing along her flexibility to her daughters and to us. Her advice for her older daughter, Malia: "I just encourage her to breathe . . . to lower the perfection bar." Her advice to other women: "Be open. Give yourself a break. Stop thinking that there is an answer to that question. Just live your life and figure out what's in your heart. What you need will change every year. And you've got to be ok with that."

Finally, Michelle Obama is both traditional and disruptive. The self-proclaimed mom-in-chief embraces cultural norms about women's reign at home. Being a mother is her first priority. And she advances societal stereotypes about men's lackluster domestic performance, making public comments about Barack's untidiness and unwillingness to chip in: "He *can* cook, but he doesn't." In many ways they are a typical couple. She tries to get him to quit smoking. He tries to get her to take bigger risks.

Like many women, Michelle Obama's early impressions about women's roles were formed at home. Marian Robinson was one of the very few stay-at-home mothers in their South Side Chicago neighborhood, a privilege that allowed her to volunteer her time and imbed in her children a strong commitment to civic engagement. But she also learned traditional ideals from society at large. Like many young girls of her era, Michelle had an Easy Bake Oven and plenty of Barbie dolls. "Barbie seemed to be the standard for perfection," she said later. "That was what the world told me to aspire to."[10] Michelle watched the same "choosy moms choose Jif" commercials that we all did, and she too was indoctrinated with the message that a woman's most important job is caregiver.

It was only later that Michelle Robinson came to believe her adult life would involve more than cooking for Ken in their dream house. For Michelle, to forgo pursuing a career would be to squander the education she and her parents worked so hard for her to attain. It also represented a huge financial risk, since her husband's career as an activist and politician was hardly a guarantee of economic freedom. After her marriage in 1992 she refused to conform to the domestic model of stay-at-home mom or socialite, always having a career separate from her husband that was stable. But the demands of working full time outside the home and being the boss inside the home took its toll. Soon she would discover, like so many of us, that our favorite TV mom sold us a bill of goods. Claire Huxtable couldn't possibly have cooked, cleaned, looked fabulous, had a delightful marriage, birthed and raised five perfectly well-behaved children . . . and made partner at a law firm. Eventually, the reality of doing it all began to create a rift in Michelle and Barack's relationship.

Early in their marriage it bothered Michelle that Barack's career took priority over hers and tension between them mounted, but instead of stewing in resentment indefinitely she decided to be the change agent in her own life, the way she had been taught. She decided to shape what was in her control. Eventually she came to realize that "I needed support. I didn't necessarily need it from Barack."[11] Michelle refused to be the working mommy martyr and began doing one of the most difficult things for working mothers: she prioritized herself. She started leaving the house at dawn to go workout, which forced her husband to take care of the girls in the morning. She built a village of friends, family and babysitters so that support would always be a text away. She learned to ask for help and no longer considered her success a solo endeavor. The combination of her traditional and disruptive personas represents a modern mantra: a good woman sacrifices, but not at her own expense.

Michelle Obama takes her job as First Lady just as seriously as any other. She sees it as another important opportunity she doesn't want to squander. "This is a rare platform and I have to use it to the best of my ability."

When you google the word "perfect" the first definition is "having all the required or desirable elements, qualities or characteristics; as good as it is possible to be." The sample sentence? *She strove to be the perfect wife.*

It took me a long time to adopt this mantra myself and to embrace my own imperfection. For the first eight years of my marriage I was not so much striving as I was on autopilot. During my childhood my mother was a homemaker and preacher's wife. My security was her pep talks, peach cobbler, and the meticulousness with which she cornrowed my sister's and my hair in the same direction. I wanted to be like her. And I was just as inspired by my mother-in-law, who left her village in Ghana as a girl to board a ship alone to London. Many years later she returned home with a nursing degree, husband, three children and an entrepreneurial spirit, eventually building the largest commercial fishing venture in the country. Her best advice to me: If things are getting easier, it's probably because you're headed downhill. Standing next to my husband on my wedding day, informed by their examples, I just assumed that my primary role as wife and mother would involve plenty of hard work, sacrifice and selflessness. Little did I know, standing under the arch, that too much of anything is peril. It took three years after having my first child for me to discover that we can achieve more by not caring which direction the clothes hangers are facing, by not apologizing with reckless abandon, by letting the mail pile up and by ordering takeout. I now know the same secret that Michelle does: in order to *have* it all we can't *do* it all.

Michelle Obama is the perfect First Lady because she is imperfect. Michelle doesn't pretend to be the perfect anything. And she admonishes women to not give in to the pressure. "We have to get off the guinea pig wheel of trying to meet other people's expectations," she told me when I met her at the White House. But she does aspire to excellence. "I wouldn't want to disappoint my parents. I wouldn't want to disappoint the country."[12]

Her complexity is her dichotomy. That is why she resonates. American society has a knack for punishing complex women. We like them to fit one mold. But because Michelle lives in the middle, no matter who you are when you look at her you see yourself.

She Slays: Michelle Obama & the Power of Dressing Like You Mean It

TANISHA C. FORD

She was a vision, bold in marigold, a marigold Narciso Rodriguez sheath dress, that is. The reality was that few had tuned into the State of the Union address to hear the words of a lame duck president. Most were in it to see First Lady Michelle Obama, "Lady O," as she is affectionately called, who dazzled from the time the camera panned up to her seat where she sat perched on high in the House of Representatives' chamber.

And she did not disappoint. Michelle waved to onlookers as her signature fringe brushed her long eyelashes, effortlessly working her Black girl magic on the crowd. Later, we would learn that she had done it again. The FLOTUS broke the internet! Her vivid sartorial confection sold out on the Neiman Marcus website before Barack Obama could even finish his final speech.

When Michelle dresses the world watches,

which is why her decision to wear a designer's garment can make him or her a household name overnight. She has helped to launch and/or elevate the careers of designers of color including Tracy Reese, Naeem Khan, Duro Olowu, and Maki Oh. And seemingly overnight, Michelle Obama has joined the pantheon of Black women actors, singers, models, and socialites who have set the world ablaze with their signature looks. What sets her apart is her participation in the tumultuous space of American politics within which she must dress and present herself to the world.

From her color palette and favorite silhouettes, to the flounce of her bangs, Mrs. Obama has become a fashion tour-de-force. Her style team ensures that every look is flawless, and she wears a variety of designers to keep her look fresh and timeless. She has covered nearly every magazine: from *Vogue* and *Ebony* to *Time* and *Fitness.* While many first ladies have been featured in magazines, the breadth and variety of Michelle's covers speak to her wide appeal. Fashion critics and industry insiders in particular have embraced Michelle as the fashion maven-in-chief. But they were merely confirming something Black women already knew: Michelle Obama is a bawse!

Clothes can only enhance what exists within the person. A true stylista has to bring something to her garments. There's no doubt, Michelle serves fierceness.

Her Black womanness matters to the millions of Black women and girls who admire her, feel protective of her, even though they've never met her. I am one of them, a Black woman professor who studies fashion in the academy — a place that does not always embrace style *or* Blackness.

In many ways, I feel our journeys run parallel: Black girls from the Midwest — her from Chicago, me from Fort Wayne, Indiana. I started my professional career while the Obamas were in office, and I was navigating some similar race and gender issues as Michelle (on a much smaller scale, of course): in what spaces were Black women's bodies allowed, how should our bodies be adorned, and what does our adornment say about our "professionalism" and our "qualifications"? Early in my career, I wore garments in vibrant prints and colors, stiletto heels, wigs, and other items that departed from the staid elbow-patched, blazer-and-bow-tie ensemble that one associates with professors. As I reached professional milestones, I celebrated the fact that I was able to do so, largely on my own terms. And of course, my professional life is unfolding as I see Michelle Obama changing the face of the American First Lady, delivering powerful speeches, and slaying photo ops. She became *my* First Lady in a way that no other First Lady had been.

Even many non-Black Americans who were skeptical about Michelle in the beginning have been won over by her humorous, straightforward-yet-loving persona, regal beauty, and political intellect. A celebrity in her own right, she manages to occupy the roles of First Lady and fashionista while also maintaining her "sista girl realness." She makes the voice of the White House one that is accessible and relatable. Black.

But her designer clothing has not protected her from racist and sexist comments about her body or problematic conversations about her personality, rooted in centuries-long stereotypes about Black women. Even though she is experiencing luxuries that most Black folks will never know, she still is not safe from social violence or threats of physical violence. It is her experience, as a Black woman who knows the pleasures and pains of being stylish while Black, that connects us to her.

Style has always mattered to Black Americans. We have been enslaved, been denied equal rights, and have been, and continue to be, the targets of state-sanctioned and vigilante violence. Clothing is a way we reclaim our humanity, express our creativity, celebrate our roots, and forge political solidarities. We style out as a mode of survival. So when and where Michelle Obama enters — dressed to the nines in Black designers such as Tracy Reese and Duro Olowu — Black women and girls enter with her. She is a symbol of many Black Americans' hopes and dreams, a symbol of our collective hurt and pain. These histories are mapped onto her five-foot-ten-inch frame.

Sure, sure, her style is reflective of the highly crafted choreography of the political world. All of her looks are planned by a team of buyers, stylists, and estheticians. This tight-lipped inner circle keeps Obama's secrets close, only sharing White House–approved information about her garments.

But I would like to believe she does indeed interject herself into the conversation. In my head, Malia and Sasha discuss fashion with their mom and help her pick out clothes as part of a mother-daughter ritual, similar to the one I had with my mother when I was growing up. For Black girls, bonding time with the women in their lives over hair and clothing are moments where they find safety and comfort, where family history is exchanged, and where they have playful conversations about what is and isn't in style anymore. Getting dressed, then, for Michelle is about more than dazzling in a publication or at a State House dinner. It is about passing on knowledge and power to a younger generation. Thus, Michelle speaks to us, Black women and girls, when she dresses. She whispers to us as she strolls red carpets, attends White House galas, and ventures out on state-sponsored trips to places as far flung as South Africa and Taiwan: your body is beautiful, do not believe the lies they tell about you, you are Black and proud.

Plus, Michelle showed us from early on that she was frank and outspoken, that she had her own opinions and was not invested in playing the political game. To me, that suggests that she would not allow someone to dress her in clothes she did not feel comfortable wearing. In fact, she told fashion industry legend Andre Leon Talley in 2009, "I love clothes . . . first and foremost, I wear what I love."

Moreover, the evolution of Michelle Obama's style over the past eight years not only suggests to me that what she wears does matter to her but that she has become a student of fashion. She clearly has a keen eye for the colors and silhouettes that flatter her statuesque body and knowledge of the designers who make them.

When I first saw Michelle Obama on *Oprah,* before Barack Obama even announced his candidacy, with her polite flipped bob, muted colors, mom flats, and conservative cuts, I did not think of her as a fashion plate. I definitely never believed she would become the style goddess that she is now. Even early on the campaign trail, she rocked dark turtlenecks and bell-sleeved jackets. Her style was a bit dated. She looked older than her years. It was clear that she cared about her appearance, probably having been schooled from a young age about the importance of leaving the house well groomed as a sign of her sense of self-dignity and promise. But as a busy high-powered professional and working wife and mother, it was clear that functionality and practicality trumped style.

Once Barack Obama became the Democratic nominee, and certainly after the Obamas won the White House, Michelle underwent a style makeover. The rationale behind the switch from her high-power professional woman ensembles to what would become her signature glammed-up mom look for the first term of Obama's presidency is a closely guarded secret. But we can look at the changes and draw conclusions about what her team was attempting to do.

Michelle's early public image ratings were low. The American public and political insiders and members of the media elite deemed her a ball buster who would not play the game, who belittled her husband and told embarrassing stories that made him look bad in public. They were speculating about whether the high-powered career woman would be another Hillary-type of First Lady who conspicuously wore her political ambitions like a well-tailored suit. Even Black folks debated what kind of First Lady Michelle would be because it was clear to us that the Princeton- and Harvard-educated Obama was capable of doing it all, if she so chose. Her team clearly decided to mold her into a twenty-first-century version of a Jackie Kennedy type of First Lady, who was impeccably dressed as she attended to hearth and home.

Like the Kennedys, the Obamas would be packaged as the young, good-looking, charismatic couple who could cut a striking pose in designer digs while effortlessly telling jokes and holding court at their White House barbeques with their new celebrity friends. They were the couple you wanted to know. You wanted to socialize with them, be in their inner circle. Like Jackie Kennedy, Michelle would not project her own political ambitions. She would be the mom-in-chief, whose primary responsibilities were to her children and the home. She would be approachable and warm. Though she was stylish, her early style was not nearly as glamorous as Jackie Kennedy's, but she started to build a name for herself in the fashion world because she wore many U.S.-based designers — ranging from Jason Wu to J. Crew.

Initially, Michelle did not have an official stylist. She was still purchasing her clothing from Chicago-based boutiques such as Ikram Goldman. It was Goldman who helped coordinate her election looks and her early First Lady style, which could be described as "soccer mom chic," the PTA mom with a makeover. In line with her mom-in-chief branding, she wore J. Crew sheath dresses, often in floral prints, satin capri pants, and kitten heel mules. Mrs. Obama mixed high with low fashions (Talbots, Zara, Thakoon), again, in an attempt to stay relevant to middle-class moms.

Her clothes early in that first term seemed to constantly try to communicate, "I am not the big bad scary Black woman; I am more like you than you think." And the clothing choices were reinforced by the narrative the White House created through television appearances and in print media. We were to believe that she had the same friends as before she became FLOTUS, that they still met and shared strategies for transporting the kids to and from soccer practice while figuring out if they should get a nanny. Team Obama even circulated pictures of Michelle shopping at Target and revealed that she secretly frequented the store, dressed down, shopping inconspicuously. She was also known to wear items more than once — a shocker! — such as her oft-recycled magenta silk chine Michael Kors dress, which she wore on election night. The March 2009 cover of *Vogue* featured Michelle delicately draped over a cream couch wearing a fuchsia sheath dress. The Annie Leibovitz–photographed spread placed Michelle in submissive poses, wearing feminine colors.

But as fashion critic Robin Givhan has noted, the genteel femininity through which we read Jackie Kennedy was not available to Michelle Obama as a Black woman. A perfect example of this is the media controversy around Obama's choice to wear garments that exposed her upper arms. Though Jackie Kennedy also wore sleeveless frocks, her milky arms were read as lithe and petite, nonthreatening. Michelle, conversely, received a far more scathing response. The conservative media went crazy, writing stories about the First Lady's arms. For them her arms were too muscular, too masculine. They were appalled by seeing the health-conscious Obama doing pushups in public to promote her anti-childhood obesity campaign Let's Move! Obama was somehow stronger and larger than life, threatening even. This fixation on her arms allowed conservative political pundits to have a conversation about the whole of her body and the ways in which it was out of place in the White House.

Americans heard these messages, which for many only justified their own long-held prejudices about Blackness. Michelle was caught in the cyclone of anti-Black racism. Conservative media outlet Fox News referred to Michelle as Barack's "baby mama," damning language that both criticized women who had children with men to whom they were not married, but also was meant to undermine Michelle's reality as wife *and* mother. It was a way to verbally punish her, to knock her back to size with racially and culturally coded language. She pressed forward despite being trapped in what Melissa Harris-Perry terms the "crooked room," or a room that is not architecturally straight; therefore, when a Black woman tries to stand erect, she cannot. But instead of the world seeing the problem with the structure of the room, it determines the problem is the Black woman with poor posture. Stereotypical media representations of the Black woman as "jezebel," "sapphire," and "mammy" are examples of the real life implications of the crooked room.

Despite, and perhaps because of, the vitriolic response to Michelle's upper arm flesh, her arms were more iconic than her fashion in that first term. Her team used this fervor to further brand Obama. They used her audacity to bare her arms as a way to position her as a more youthful, more in touch with trends, cooler, and more transgressive First Lady than Hillary and the Bushes. She was a new-millennium First Lady. At some point, the team stopped trying to assuage Americans' fears of her Blackness and started reminding people that she was a bad ass, and she had the "guns" to prove it.

Team Obama began to acknowledge that she was not like the other First Ladies and that her Blackness *did* make her different. For example, by virtue of her skin tone, she ushered in new trends for First Lady fashions. She opted to wear colors that deviated from the standard political color palette, choosing bold colors that looked good on Black skin. Where most first ladies wore reds, blues, and pastels, Obama mixed these colors with vibrant pinks and rich jewel tones. Why should she try to fit the demure mold of other, white First Ladies, when historically the claim to femininity and the protection that came with it wasn't afforded to Black women? Michelle Obama found a way to work within the demands of the office of First Lady while transgressing these same norms.

We, as Black women, respected and admired how she lived between these two tensions: the stature and visibility of the office of First Lady and the disturbing social responses to her Black womanness. We could relate to the range of questions we imagined folks in the political world asked her, based on the questions our own colleagues and classmates asked us about our hair and our culture. Even though her platform was larger than ours, her daily routine — with her team of secret service agents who clocked and coordinated her every move — different than ours, she was us. Even if she was the First Lady, first and foremost, she was a Black woman, and no one would let her forget that. And she seemed to never forget that herself.

This new Michelle brand, which had no historical precedents, played well with millennials especially, and her public opinion ratings started to climb. According to Gallup, her approval ratings topped Barack Obama's. This was in part due to her frequent media appearances, powerful celebrity friends (including Beyoncé), and her style, which was becoming edgier as the Obamas neared the second campaign. In short, the Obamas had become the darlings of American popular culture. They had transcended politics. They were bonafide celebrities. That "we're just like you, America . . . only a bit cooler" shtick that marked the early first term no longer played. Michelle's new look for President Obama's second term was a reflection of their new status as cultural icons.

She had some nice fashion "moments" in the first four years, but in the second term, she clearly announced that she came to slay!

She and her team started taking major risks, and her style explicitly referenced working-class Black American sartorial traditions. No longer was she seeking to blend in, she was making jaw-dropping fashion statements. Her earrings and other accessories became more opulent, her outfits more fitted, her hair more bouffant. She proved that she still had a lot of "South Side Chi" in her!

Right before the 2013 inauguration, Michelle debuted new bangs for her forty-ninth birthday, which set the tone for the second term. Her hairstylist Johnny Wright created a modern, softer take on the fringe bob, which elevated her look from soccer mom to cosmopolitan stylista. At the inauguration she paired her new hair with a silk Thom Browne jacquard dress, an embellished J. Crew waist belt, Reed Krakoff suede boots, and fuchsia leather gloves. As her bestie Beyoncé belted out the "Star Spangled Banner," Michelle ushered in a new era of Obama style in which she would solidify herself as the fashionable First Lady, rivaling Jackie Kennedy for the crown.

Looking more youthful the older she gets, Obama takes more fashion risks as she no longer has to prove to the American public that she is who she says she is. Besides, her comical "evolution of the mom dance" skit on *Late Night with Jimmy Fallon* pretty much bodied all of her critics. Moreover, as the body positive and curvy body movement has grown in popularity, Michelle and team have started showing off her curves. While A-lined dresses were a main staple in the first term, she has increasingly worn garments that are cinched at the waist to accentuate her curvy figure or risqué looks such as the off-the-shoulder fitted Zac Posen bustier dress she wore to Black Girls Rock! in 2015. The side-swept hair that hung past her shoulders and the black Vera Wang fitted mermaid gown at the state dinner with the president of China is another example of her edgier look. I remember watching the news footage and thinking, "President Obama looks like he's got a young thang on his arm!," as she leaned in to straighten his bowtie (one of their classic "cool kid" moves).

Michelle Obama has forever changed the possibilities of the position of FLOTUS. Designers clamor to dress her. She even sports looks straight off the runway, such as the Derek Lam suede patchwork dress she wore to Beijing in 2014. She has created a new color palette for First Ladies and has made wearing one's arms out cool for women over forty. But the thing that true fashionistas know is that clothes are just clothes on an unconfident body. One must embody style and attitude in order for the looks to make an impact. Because of Michelle's reality as a Black woman, she shifted the conversation about dress, about beauty, and body. But of course, we as Black women been knowing that Michelle Obama was magic.

Cooking with a Narrative
MARCUS SAMUELSSON

Both Michelle and her mom, for me, have established this base level of abnormal normalcy during the Obama presidency. I look at them as a family, a Black family in that big White House. As the First Lady, Michelle was challenged with raising her daughters in very important years in the White House, in front of everybody. A grandmother plays a critical part in that White House, to establish normalcy. I was raised just a bike ride away from my grandmother so I know how vital that bond can be. She's the person who you can turn to and say, "School wasn't great today, or I had a fight with this guy" or other stuff that we all go through.

When I've visited that house, Michelle's mother has almost always been there. She's yelling at the dog or grabbing the kids. This is a big house, of course, but she's adding that level of presence. She reminds you,

"This is a real house. A family lives here."

They never budged on being a Black family. It means that we're together, and we're raising this tribe, this village together. I'm sure they had a nanny, but it wasn't about the nanny first. It was about Grandma first, and establishing some values and deep roots in a very front and center environment. Their values of being the family from Chicago didn't change because they moved to D.C. Even with that level of everyday intensity, she didn't change, and I love that. Wow. Who's done *that* before?

Then you put that family element in the context of their being the first Black family in the White House, and you look at her choices after the election. I think those choices led her to me. I don't think she would have thought about the garden and food if the kids had been 22 and out of the house. Eating right becomes really real when your family's growing up. Because she is the First Lady, especially in this day and age, everything you do becomes a microphone for what you say.

When she chose to put in the garden, I remember thinking, "Yes! She's picking food." It could have been anything. It could have been growing flowers. It could have been bike riding. It could have been reading. It could have been swimming, which are all amazing causes for young families to know more about, but she picked us — the food community.

I think one of the reasons why the chef community came out in such full support of her is because she picked a topic and a dialogue that let the world know she wanted to talk to us. We could help her help the kids and generate this incredible wind of excitement for Americans. That was a big deal. She's talking to us! Her work was our chance to open the door and get included in the conversation.

The other thing that I love about the First Lady is how transformative she's been in helping the world see Black beauty. When they started to talk about, "her arms are so beautiful" or "her skin is so beautiful," that was also a way of saying, "Yeah, there's a new normal of how people can look and feel and be." We look different, and we're proud of it, and we're not going to try to put a blush on it and be a little bit blonder or a little bit — no. We're rocking this Blackness.

In terms of fashion, she brought in Jason Wu. She brought in Duro Olowu. She brought in an element that said, "I'm a Black woman. I'm gorgeous, and I'm not going to try to look and feel different in form. The color patterns are different. The hairstyles are different. The arms cut is different. The length of the skirt, how it falls, is different." She never tried, "Oh, I think I should fit in a Chanel and it should be a certain size." No. She said, "I'm rocking this body, this skin, this hair and I'm rocking it hard."

When I see her, when I'm in her presence, she is, to me, fierce in the way you think of an Annie Lennox or an athlete like Serena Williams or a writer like Maya Angelou was. Michelle Obama is someone that is fierce in the smartest, most intelligent way. She has this incredible balance of understanding Chicago and the world and the street, but also understanding corporate America and understanding as a woman, as a Black woman, how she has to articulate and package that in order to reach the furthest scope of humanity. That is a window into an intellect that is so different from Jackie or Nancy or Barbara, which doesn't mean that they weren't intelligent. But I know how hard it is, as a person of color, and being a Black woman, to be so in control of the image you are portraying to the world.

She's not just trying to communicate to people in D.C. or Chicago or New York. She knows: "Whatever I say, it's going to reach Japan and back on Twitter and on Instagram." It means that every sigh, every facial expression, is analyzed. If I'm not looking at you long enough, I'm arrogant. Other First Ladies didn't have to contend with Instagram. Or Twitter. We couldn't travel as fast, so for her to do that, whether she was on *Ellen* or David Letterman or Jimmy Fallon or CNN, and every single time, come away with, "Holy shit. She's great." That's not easy.

It's stunning. It's nothing short of stunning the way she manages a 24/7 news cycle.

It's an amazing achievement, for her to be so relevant in those conversations, whether it's talking about Obamacare or talking about New York Fashion Week or kids' food. Always aware that, no matter what she says, she's speaking to the world. She is putting something out there to the world that the world has never seen before.

When you think about what she represents, it's almost Mandela-esque. If you're a Black girl in Africa and you're told that you can only go to school to second year. Then you have someone in your image, you see a Michelle Obama, her very existence represents a path and it represents possibility. She tells African girls: this means you can vote. This means you can get a job. This means you can be a lawyer. This means you can go to an Ivy League school. This means that you can win a scholarship. This means that you can raise a family. This means that you can really transform yourself.

She represents, on a global stage, door after door after door opening and possibility, just by her mere existence.

I came to my true identity as an African, late. It was later in the game. Obama searched for his African heritage and wrote about it in his book. What I love is I don't think his Africanism is anything she would ever have wanted him to trade away. The vibe I get is, "We are truly African-American, with a foot or a toe or a hand in the continent." I think that's also why the hope in the continent is so much for them, and the love for Obama in the continent is so strong, because there is a direct linkage. I think that's something that will never go away.

I first met them when he was running for Senator and came to New York. We spoke a few times.

It's so funny. I still have his old number in my phone, his Chicago number.

I still have that 312 number.

I've had it for all those years, from back in the day. It's vintage!

When Sam Kass, who had worked for the Obamas as a personal chef and followed them to the White House, asked me to be one of the chefs considered to cook the first state dinner, he was very clear: "The garden means something. We're going to do something around it." I started to think about the fact that the state dinners have never been about American food. If you have a garden, let's pick vegetables from the garden and cook from that. The fact that it was to honor Indian Prime Minister Manmohan Singh and he's a vegetarian, let's show some compassion and respect to that. I thought, whether you pick my menu or not, it will help you think about what you serve in the most meaningful way.

Then Andrea from my team started to go down to Washington to work with me. Andrea told me that during these tastings, Michelle was very present. The dog was very present. The kids were very present. She said, "It's like you're in someone's home, but you're dealing with the First Lady and the family."

That helped me see things differently. I thought, I can't think about it as the White House. I've got to think about, we're doing a party, a big party for a family. They are throwing a party for 400 people in a very gracious home, versus thinking about the state and city, and country. It made it more homey. It was a lighter touch point, it was a better reference point than thinking about the first state dinner, and the pressure that comes with that.

When you cook around something that is so big, you can get nervous. My staff could be a little bit nervous, but I couldn't be nervous. So I thought, I'm just cooking with this great family.

I wanted to bring being African and being Black into the menu. I wanted to cook collards and cornbread, put that on the very first state dinner menu. I wanted the meal to read as a story of migration. We wouldn't put that aside. I wanted to write a menu that said to the world, "We can be thoughtful. We can be American, and come from us, by us, for us, but it's for everyone." We put the collards in. We put the cornbread in.

It was easier for me as a chef to craft that narrative than it would have been for her as First Lady. But she okayed it; then it was on.

There were a lot of things that had never happened before. There's never been a bread course. I thought: What would be better than for 400 people who really didn't know each other to be able to pass the bread? Now we're breaking bread. Cornbread and chapati, very Indian, very American. Like pickles and achar, some American, some very Indian. I was just imagining these dishes in conversation with each other.

I felt like shrimp from New Orleans was the right choice. It was right after the BP scandal, so it was important to say, "We're buying our seafood from New Orleans." We have cornbread. We have collards, this very American show-and-tell, but not the obvious stuff. That is very American to me. Showing in a very soft way, we're going to start this off right.

This is how we set the tone.

That's what hospitality comes down to. I've cooked for so many presidents and kings and queens, but this is something where I emotionally feel very, very connected.

We served okra, of course, and chickpeas, that felt very Indian to me. We knew we'd serve rice, but how did rice come to this country? Through the slave trade, and in Washington, D.C., you're very close to Virginia. All of that history is right there. Right there! D.C.'s really the last stop or the first stop of that slave route, depending on which direction you were going.

The migration story was very much at the heart of the menu I created for the state dinner. Cooking with a narrative is something that's possible for every family; it's as relevant for Sunday supper as it is for a state dinner. You can own that in whatever capacity you want. Let what you serve be a way of connecting: you cook and all of a sudden, you're connecting to your college year in New Orleans, or now you're connecting to your crazy cousin in California. Now you're connecting to your auntie in Chicago. It's cooking with a narrative, the way we keep telling our story. Feeding itself is pretty flat and boring, but eating with a spiritual compass and cooking with a narrative is what's going to connect us, especially since our day-to-day life is so different from the way our parents and our grandparents lived.

In Sweden, I grew up with Canadian cousins. When they came back with something from Quebec, it could have been maple syrup, that was their way of saying, "We missed you guys. We know you can't get maple syrup." It's cooking with a narrative. No family story's better or bigger than anyone else's. This is important. Being an immigrant in this country is being challenged. Being different is being challenged. Don't let them take your story away from you. Hold on to Honduras, Ethiopia, England, Miami, whatever it might be. Music and cooking might be the two strongest ways of connecting to who we are and where we come from. We are all Americans, of course, but dig into the places you've come from. This is what makes you you. That's the new version of soul.

After the State dinner, Michelle Obama invited me to cook at the Easter Egg hunt. I saw her every year and every year, she grew. You could see she was a person who got more comfortable in her setting. She grew, and I loved seeing her grow. By my third visit to the White House, it was clear, it's her house now. It's her house. "What are you doing? You're in my house." I just kept cheering for her: "Good for you. Take it. It's yours. Good."

Cooking with her on *Good Morning America,* she has a sense of joy around her. You get happy when you see her. She always whispers something to me about what her next food plan is, "We're doing this." That whisper is something, as Black people, we understand. You don't strut when you've got real power, real power whispers.

When we look at her legacy, we will see

how she opened up this whole idea about the democratization of food. In Harlem, we now have six farmers' markets. We wouldn't have six farmers' markets if there hadn't been a top-level-driven and a local-level-driven conversation with her at its heart.

When she does a video parody of Lil Jon called "Turnip for What," it shows that she understands her time, the speed and power of the internet. She's not afraid of uploading her message on Vine or Twitter. A lot of politicians have been afraid of social media, but she says, "This medium is not just going to go against us. I can also use this medium to push messages out." Through Instagram and her many channels of communicating, she puts it out there. Then people can respond to *her* version of her story.

That is completely new for a Black person in the spotlight and for a Black woman, especially. For so long we were told what to do, how to look, how to feel and even how to be. Her control of social media is so powerful. Rather than merely responding and reacting, she shapes the conversation. She says, "No, this is how it is."

I think she embodies the ability to shape the conversation around her better than any person that I know. She took a minute to assess the lay of the land. Then she said,

"You know what? Enough. This is how I'm going to shape it, how I'm going to look, how I'm going to raise my family. How I'm going to communicate with you. This is how I'm going to show who I am and what I can be and where I'm going. Boom, boom, boom. I'm setting the flag down here."

STATE DINNER

In Honor of
HIS EXCELLENCY
DR. MANMOHAN SINGH
PRIME MINISTER OF THE
REPUBLIC OF INDIA
and
MRS. GURSHARAN KAUR

Dinner Menu

Potato and Eggplant Salad
White House Arugula
With Onion Seed Vinaigrette

*2008 Sauvignon Blanc, Modus Operandi,
Napa Valley, California*

Red Lentil Soup with Fresh Cheese

*2006 Riesling, Brooks "Ara,"
Willamette Valley, Oregon*

Roasted Potato Dumplings
With Tomato Chutney
Chick Peas and Okra
or
Green Curry Prawns Caramelized Salsify
With Smoked Collard Greens and
Coconut Aged Basmati

*2007 Granache, Beckmen Vineyards,
Santa Ynez, California*

Pumpkin Pie Tart Pear Tatin
Whipped Cream and Caramel Sauce

*Sparkling Chardonnay, Thibaut-Janisson
Brut, Monticello, Virginia*

Petits Fours and Coffee Cashew Brittle
Pecan Pralines
Passion Fruit and Vanilla Gelees
Chocolate-Dipped Fruit

MICHELLE OBAMA: REPRESENTATIONAL JUSTICE

SARAH LEWIS

During the Civil War, the abolitionist and great nineteenth-century thinker Frederick Douglass made a surprising speech about the importance of pictures for justice. It was the dawn of the photographic age. In the speech, which he rewrote multiple times, Douglass argued that combat might end complete sectional disunion, but America's progress and racial reconciliation would require pictures because of the images they conjure in one's imagination. Douglass was making a case for the epiphanic power of an image to shift our vision of the world. He was making a case for the power of an image to arrest us, to penetrate us, to stop us in our tracks.

Resolute as Douglass was, he ended his speech with an admission — he thought it might take generations to understand the power of images to shift our vision for this country. Centuries later, we would have an example of the impact of pictures that he had in mind.

"I wake up every day in a house built by slaves," Michelle Obama told the crowd at the City College of New York in 2016. She continued to emphasize the point: "I watch my daughters — two beautiful, Black young women — head off to school, waving good-bye to their father, the president of the United States, the son of a man from Kenya who came here to America." The power of the sentence was completed by her image — an African American woman, descendant of those brought here in bondage, serving as the First Lady of the United States. She didn't have to state that about her own history. By then, we all already knew.

Over time the image of Michelle Obama had become a colossus, a towering figure into which fell the opportunity, challenge, and contradiction of Blackness, power, and beauty. The intense visual study went beyond the scrutiny historically received by First Ladies. Our collective gaze became an assessment that exposed the very core of our nation's stereotypes and racial views.

She was aware of the transformation from the beginning. "When my husband first started campaigning for President, folks had all sorts of questions of me," she said. "Was

I too loud, or too angry, or too emasculating? Or was I too soft, too much of a mom, not enough of a career woman? Then there was the first time I was on a magazine cover — it was a cartoon drawing of me with a huge afro and machine gun. Now, yeah, it was satire, but if I'm really being honest, it knocked me back a bit. It made me wonder, just how are people seeing me."[1]

I first saw Michelle Obama as if she was watching herself be true to a self-made pact of utter authenticity — convicted, self-possessed, forthright. "My view on this stuff is I'm trying to be myself, trying to be as authentic as I can be. I can't pretend to be somebody else," she said in 2007.[2] She stated it again a year later with the words "trying to be" as if a near refrain. "I am trying to be as authentically me as I can be," she mentioned in 2008.[3]

To some, the phrase might have been confusing. Michelle Obama seemed to be someone for whom there is no try, there is only do and do not. Accomplishment is her image. Indeed, there she was — casually curled on the couch, making lists, about to move into the White House — in front of Annie Leibovitz's lens for *Vogue.* Yet the phrase let slip her knowledge about the examinations she was enduring — from the public, from the press — that were not so much about her, but about why we had never seen someone like her before as a potential First Lady of the United States of America.

Authenticity is not an achievement. Yet authenticity does take effort if you are upending centuries of history with your mere presence. It takes work to let people stare, wonder, probe and prod to determine the veracity of your life. It does involve some "try." It takes effort to convince the world that you are authentic when simply being you shatters the mold. Images that create the dominant cultural narratives about African American life rarely show a life like Michelle Obama's. It created an oxymoron: authenticity became a declarative act.

International curiosity turned the image of Michelle Obama into a public figurative emblem, an iconic image in the frieze of American landmark images of race and representation. "My life isn't new, but it's new to a lot of people who haven't seen this up close and personal," she would reflect years later, as if explaining the figurative tour America took of her body, her life, and her lineage.[4]

As a professor of History of Art and Architecture and African and African American Studies at Harvard, I spend my time thinking about the nexus of vision, race, and representation. Yet the repeated image of Michelle Obama in the public eye turned looking into our collective work.

I understood this when I received a call from a journalist writing a major piece on Black professionals on a mid-winter afternoon in 2008. He wanted to know about my life. He started asking about my other friends and colleagues who were Black and driven. I paused and asked, "What is the focus of this story?" The democratic race involving then candidate Barack Obama had put a spotlight on pioneering Black professionals. As the interview went on, I realized that the story seemed to be less about Black professionals and more about why people are suddenly aware of and interested in our achievements. He was asking me for a figurative tour. The journalist never ran the piece. He admitted during our call, with humility and self-reflection that I deeply admired, that he was interviewing subjects, but he really could have been interviewing himself.

If Black professionals of pedigree had become news, Michelle Obama as the potential First Lady of the United States was exploding the mold. "I will walk anyone through my life," she would say.[5] And she did, donating her body to the nation's gaze for constant assessment for us all.

As Robin Givhan put it, "The rise of First Lady Michelle Obama as an icon — of fashion, black womanhood, working motherhood and middle-class success — has propelled her onto a pedestal that would surely give the average person vertigo. She is Jackie Kennedy, Sojourner Truth, Hillary Clinton and a Horatio Alger character all rolled into one."[6] Deborah Willis amplified the comment when she observed that Michelle Obama "has engaged the imagination of a new generation of writers and artists as they chronicle the commanding role the First lady now plays in American *visual* culture."[7]

It took my mind back centuries.

I read that Michelle Obama's friend said, "she's a private person in a public role, a black woman in a costume drama previously only played by whites" and I imagined how she had reversed the racially symbolic production — the Masque of Blackness commissioned by King James at the birth of the so-called New World.[8] In this masque in 1604, Queen Anne and her ladies had completely covered themselves in black paint to perform as princesses from the

172

River Niger come to Britain to be cleansed of their Blackness. It scandalized the court. Centuries later, the image of Michelle Obama had indeed reversed the costume drama. She had fully upended the masque of Blackness on American soil.

I wondered how many knew that Black beauty once contained the incendiary power of a detonation. In the nineteenth century, just after emancipation, Winslow Homer, then America's best-known painter, was nearly forced out of his hotel at gunpoint and called a racial epithet for deigning to show Blackness as beautiful with paint. At the time, Homer was in Virginia painting works of African Americans including *The Cotton Pickers* (1876), a portrait of two African American enslaved women rendered with a rare grace and dignity. Homer agreed to hold an informal exhibit of his recently completed portraits in the lobby of his hotel, where one high-society lady asked, "Why don't you paint our lovely girls instead of those dreadful creatures?" Homer insisted on the beauty of his Black subjects. He replied, "Because those are the purtiest." The following day, one man came to the hotel with a shotgun looking for the "damn _____ painter." In a letter to his brother Homer said that he "looked him in

173

the eyes, as mother used to tell us to look at a wild cow." Homer's defiance worked. "Halfway to the porch [he] hesitated, then turned and rode away."[9]

Homer continued to paint African Americans for the duration of his time in Virginia, adding to a record of rare images filled with such humanity and dignity in a sea of racist caricature that Alain Locke, as late as 1940, remarked that "Homer is chiefly responsible for the modern revival of interest in the Negro subject."[10]

At the unveiling of Artis Lane's bust of Sojourner Truth, I watched as Michelle Obama spoke and wondered how many knew that she was scraping off layers of encrusted bias and history by daring to be herself in public, that she had to contend with the weight of the history of race and representation that mandated that effort.

The struggle to affirm the dignity and humanity of all cannot be waged without pictures. Race turns looking into work.

It was what Douglass knew. It is why, I have to imagine, he spent such time focusing on the nexus of race, imagery, and citizenship and spoke about the force of pictures at length in 1854, the year of the release of the widely known antebellum racial treatise *Types of Mankind,* by Josiah

Clark Nott and George Gliddon. The book presented a hierarchy of human races and polygenesis. A few years earlier, in 1850, leading naturalist Louis Agassiz had commissioned photographer J. T. Zealy to take daguerreotypes of bare-chested and bare-breasted African- and American-born slaves in South Carolina in an attempt to prove his polygenesis views. As Sean Ross Meehan writes, Douglass was arguing that pictures, the same medium that was being used to excise African Americans from the human family, could be subversively used "to read him back in."[11]

"In the making of our Presidents, the political gallery begins the operation and the picture gallery ends it," Douglass said. Centuries later, we see it with the image of First Lady Michelle Obama, a figure of representational justice, a corrective model, a demonstration of the force of repeated images to continue the journey toward full citizenship for all on American soil.

Douglass was ahead of his time.

THE FREEDOM TO BE YOURSELF
KAREN HILL ANTON

THE TOP OF THE MOUNTAIN

When I was growing up, a First Lady was just that. A lady. A woman who wore hats and smiled. Sometimes she waved a gloved hand. That's my basic image of the women who were in your role before you. I can think of only one First Lady who left an impression on me. Jackie Kennedy stood out because of her glamour and style, her presence. Still, it would have never occurred to me to want to look like her, dress like her, be like her. You changed that. You changed a lot of things and I suspect that it will only be with time that we will fully be able to appreciate the legacy of your work and your husband's presidency.

I left the United States for the first time when I was 19 years old and traveled for one year, mostly in Europe. I returned home in the early 1970s to find an America I no longer recognized. My family had moved from our apartment and community, a place where we knew everyone by name, to a housing project. My father had served as head of the Community League of 159th Street numerous times, actively participating in creating a neighborhood where the end-of-summer block party was the biggest event of our young lives, kids played outside until the streetlights came on, and keeping an eye on a neighbor's child was like keeping an eye on your own. This new place was an alien landscape, devastated by drugs and violence. It was a place I wanted no part of, a place where I would not contemplate raising a family. When I got older and my partner and I did start a family, we moved to Vermont. There, we were able to find good jobs and a wonderful school for our daughter. We would probably still be there today if Billy hadn't been offered the opportunity to study and live in Japan at a yoga training center where natural foods, meditation, and a simple healthy lifestyle were the center of the curriculum.

I have three daughters and a son. Our eldest daughter was born in Denmark, the other three children here in Japan. I've never used the term "expatriates" to describe my family and myself. My husband Billy and I, friends since we were teenagers, came to

Japan in 1975. We just never left.

Forty years ago, we arrived in Japan, and moved into a farmhouse that we would call home for nearly a decade. Stepping out of the car at what seemed to be the top of the world, I knew I'd found the place in Japan I wanted to be. I'm not sure what it was, the old house or the view, which is not quite the word one wants for a panorama of bamboo groves, tea plantations, rice fields, mountains upon mountains, and endless sky. This unknown, strange place had been waiting for us to come to it.

"This is it, Billy," I said.

"Yeah. This is it."

It was called Futokoro Yama, which loosely translated means Breastpocket Mountain. In that old house we sat on zabuton, the thick floor cushions, because there were no chairs; heated the bath with wood, because that's how we could make it hot. Our closest neighbors were the Ishikawa family. Almost all the families in that area shared the same name. The eldest Ishikawa, a man of perhaps sixty who looked seventy, made his presence known our first morning by piling up a load of wood in our yard. We were grateful and did not mention the noise had woken us up before the sun.

All throughout Japan, forty years ago

when we first arrived and to this day, rural families live like the Ishikawas with children, parents, grandparents, perhaps an aunt or uncle, all under one roof. Japanese do not view autonomy as we do, and privacy is not prized in the same way. Even with paper-thin walls, shared family life is viewed for its benefits. Michelle, I was happy to learn your mother, the esteemed Marian Robinson, would move into the White House with all of you; it was a very important moment for me because it made me realize that yours was a family that I could not only respect, but relate to. Multigenerational households are one of the things I've liked most about traditional Japanese family life. While raising our family in a small village here, ours was the only family that could go by that uncomfortable name "nuclear." We were not fortunate enough to have grand-parents to share in our children's lives, but I surely saw the value in it, and clearly you do, too.

We must all decide when and how we will make a life. We are all, in our own way, climbing a mountain. I can only imagine that your husband's presidency and your family becoming the First Family was also a climb. As I watched you from afar — 6,296 miles away to be exact — I marveled at the

patience and grace with which you under-
took the task of becoming the First Lady.
Everything about you seemed to say, "I am
going to do this. But I am going to do this
my way." What I have seen is that you
decided, as I did, that life is too short to
dispel too much energy on other people's
ignorance and the limitations that they
might prescribe. Instead, you forged your
own path. As you have said, "Success is only
meaningful and enjoyable if it feels like your
own."

A COUNTRY WITHOUT GUNS

When I moved into that century-old farmhouse on top of a mountain in central
Japan, I wondered how our family would
adjust. Would I be able to communicate
with my neighbors (all three of them)? Was
I really going to be able to build a fire to
heat the ritual nightly bath? My husband
was starting a new job, our daughter a new
school. Would she learn Japanese? There was
a lot for me to learn. And among that new
learning was that the most important thing
expected of me in my community was co-
operation. Being interdependent is a natural
state for families and society. My neighbors
accepted me, no doubt because I accepted
them.

As you become a grown-up, in the deepest sense of the word, you discover that every choice involves gains and losses. Everything is a compromise, especially in a country like Japan, where the good of the whole outweighs the good of the individual. For me, the gains were monumental. As America mourns what has become a season of unchecked gun violence, I am most grateful for the fact that I live in a country where it would be front-page news if a policeman even took his gun out of its holster.

I know you remember (the whole world does) when Barack said that if he had a son, he would look like Trayvon Martin — implying he would fear for his son's safety, and his son's life.

I have a son. I have never, ever, in all the years we've lived in Japan, worried about his or any of our children's safety. I'm talking about my girls walking home alone from ballet classes in the evenings. I'm talking about Mario, at ten years old, going to visit a friend in Osaka two hours away on a high-speed train, with a note pinned to his T-shirt and $100 in cash in his pocket. I'm forever grateful my children had that kind of childhood. It's the childhood I'd wish for all children. I loved taking our children on visits to America so they could see that we truly have a rainbow nation. But Michelle, they could not enjoy the freedom they've always had in Japan, and I disliked having the role of the admonisher: *don't go there, be careful of that, be sure and check if . . .*

I'm sure you know that handguns are illegal in Japan. Virtually no one is allowed to possess one. But what you don't know is that my neighbors ask me, as if I, because I'm American, could somehow produce a reasonable answer: *How can it be possible for Americans to have guns?* They're incredulous.

I can probably recite the Second Amendment by heart. I could explain it to them. But I doubt their question would change. In 2013 Japan recorded 0 gun deaths.

Michelle, I know you've taken a sincere interest in the health and well-being of American children. And I sincerely commend you for the changes you've effected. Still, it upsets me, and I bet you too, to think of the danger children face on a daily basis in communities across America. Walking to school, sitting on a porch, lying on a bed reading, going to the store, can all be daily activities that end in a tragic "incident" as a bullet (stray, intended, accidental — does it matter?) tears through kids' young bodies. If this isn't a public health crisis I truly don't know what is.

Whenever there's a mass shooting in the States I can see my Japanese neighbors are pained to even mention it. And I assure you mass shootings are the only ones my neighbors know about because they are reported in the Japanese news. They have no idea of the number of people who are killed in Chicago or Omaha or Baltimore on a regular basis. My neighbors are embarrassed for me. Because I'm American.

The proliferation of and easy accessibility to guns in the United States — factually easier to obtain than many mundane items — is an aberration of a modern society. Here, possession of handguns was banned in 1965 and there are strict penalties for violations. Before you can obtain a rifle for hunting, the police will first interview your family members to find out if there's any domestic strife. They'll talk to your neighbors. They will go to your job. You'll be required to have a physical and mental examination. You will have to go to a firing range to show you know how to use your weapon, and your home will be inspected to see if you know how to store it.

Yes, these steps are repressive. But here it's considered common sense to put the well-being of the society first. From this

183

perspective, what we Americans call "rights" could be called irresponsibility. Seeing the daily carnage as a consequence of the proliferation of guns, from Japan, it appears Americans exact a heavy price for their so-called "freedoms."

THE THINGS I MISS

For many years I was a columnist for *The Japan Times*. My columns covered the challenges of cross-cultural communication, the misunderstandings that may occur, the frustrations that can result. I wrote about food and exchanging recipes, and sometimes actual dishes, with my friends and neighbors. I told readers that when I went to the States I loved that I could eat corn on the cob and black cherries to my heart's content, because they're not as expensive as they are here. Readers knew that I returned to Japan like a pack horse, my luggage overweight with black-eyed peas, great northern beans, lima beans, maple syrup. When I wrote about my love for collard greens, and how much I missed them, one reader sent me collard green seeds, and another, writing from Hawaii, told me she would cook me up a pot of greens if I were ever to visit. I did, and she did.

In several columns I wrote about preparing *obento* (lunch boxes), which is serious business in Japan. It is expected your child's school *obento* is healthy, tasty, and looks attractive. My children held me to a strict standard, and youngest daughter Lila would often draw diagrams for the *obento* layout!

I loved reading about the vegetable garden you planted in the White House, the first garden on those grounds since the Victory Gardens of World War 2. I truly admired the fact that you made it a quest to make healthier foods more accessible to all Americans. I have long appreciated the connection between good nutrition and good health, and indeed it was part of what built the bridge between America and Japan for me and my husband. Billy was one of the early members of the health foods movement in America in the mid-60s, and concern for our children's and all children's health was central to our lives. The summer before we left the U.S. Billy was asked to be head chef at a camp for disadvantaged children from New York City. Preparing healthy, simple food, based on the macrobiotic diet, we (I was his sous-chef) introduced the children (some clearly malnourished) to healthy foods. Ever curious, we were delighted the children would come into the kitchen to ask questions about what we were preparing, or have a new taste experience, sampling things like Japanese seaweed, burdock root, fresh tofu. We taught them the Japanese concept of *hara hachibu* — meaning that one should only eat until the stomach is 80 percent full, and stop. Everyone in Japan is familiar with this saying, and no doubt it contributes to the fact that obesity is still rare here.

Your Japanese Counterpart, Crown Princess Masako

Like women everywhere, women in Japan need role models. You've probably met Crown Princess Masako, and I'm sure you found her to be a remarkable woman. Raised internationally, she is multilingual, received a fine education and had a rising career as a diplomat. Just like you were able to bring your professional experience and accomplishments to enhance your role as First Lady, Masako Owada definitely represented a model of success for women in Japan (and that includes my daughters) who genuinely admired and respected her. But once she entered the Imperial Household, she was reduced to the pressures of providing the country with not just an heir, but a male heir. It was unthinkable that she should play any role on the international stage other than consort to the Crown Prince. The Imperial Household is an ancient and thoroughly fossilized institution. No one expects it to change. There is an expression in Japanese, *shouganai,* that could be translated as "it can't be helped" or "it's inevitable." This pretty much sums up the national attitude toward unfortunate situations. When it had been made abundantly clear that Crown Princess Masako would not be permitted to step out of her antiquated and rigidly prescribed centuries-old role, I'm sure I heard, not a collective *shouganai,* but a national sigh of disappointment.

At the same time, my daughters have found powerful role models in the women of Japan. I was hardly surprised when I was once asked point-blank: "Aren't you worried your daughters will become like Japanese women?" The American woman who put that question to me clearly thought that was the worst thing that could happen to them. I didn't.

You see, Michelle, I didn't share this woman's view that my daughters — Nanao, Mie, and Lila — might be lesser women, somehow, if indeed they acquired whatever might be considered typical characteristics of whatever might be the typical "Japanese woman." Just as you, and of course many black women, have suffered prejudice and bias for being who you are and having assumptions made about you, there are an abundance of stereotypes about Japanese women that don't ring true. The qualities that characterize the Japanese women I know are intelligence, competence, selflessness, grace, perseverance, generosity, modesty, humility. I always thought my daughters could have worse examples to emulate. So could I.

THE FREEDOM TO BE YOURSELF

I remember once telephoning a store, here in Japan, to say that I'd be coming in to pick up an item I'd ordered. To refresh the salesperson's memory, I said "I'm the *kokujin*" — which means black person. The salesperson responded: "Oh yes, you're the foreign woman from Tenryu. We'll hold your item for you." I realized then and there that I could drop the baggage of labeling myself as a color.

Although Barack Obama becoming president was truly historic, I can't help but think what it would have been like, and how it would have been different, for you to be able to enter the White House just as the First Lady — and not the qualifying "first

African American First Lady."

Living in Japan all these years, I've found that I could let go of the "yoke of color" and what a relief that is. To just be a human being. Here our family is referred to as foreigners. Specifically, Americans. The minute we land in America and go through passport control Billy and I are looked on as an "interracial couple" and our children become an abridged "Black."

The last time you visited Japan, I actually thought I might be invited to meet you. It wasn't just wishful thinking, or delusions of self-importance. A good friend was an advisor to the United States ambassador to Japan, Caroline Kennedy. He told me that when she was confirmed as ambassador, he'd given her my name as a person in Japan she might find valuable to contact.

Well, I didn't make it on the guest list of dignitaries and distinguished expats you surely met while she was here. But, oh, Michelle, I would have loved to talk to you. I wish I could have invited you to our home. It's not in super-hip Tokyo or don't-miss Kyoto, but in the countryside of Shizuoka. Like all Japanese welcoming visitors, I would have been happy to share with you the best our region has to offer: green tea, *shiitake, mikan* — and magnificent views of

Mt. Fuji. From our home we can see bamboo groves, pine forests, and the horizon of the Pacific Ocean. I would have liked you to meet my family. You'd see that just like you, I have strived to create a family that is harmonious, loving, caring, and achieving. I would have liked to have shared a pot of tea with you and talked about the art of composing a life.

Michelle, what I really like about you is that you did not settle for an assigned role. I imagine you saw early on the potential of the position of First Lady, and determined to use it to full advantage. I guess you also saw the risks, but went for it anyhow. Wow.

Michelle, I know your father was an important and beloved figure in your life, and that his memory serves as daily motivation for you. My father too was the center of my life. He was born into a poor family in Mississippi; I don't have to tell you he faced adversity. But he prevailed, raising my brother, sister, and me as a single father. When we were growing up, he'd gather children in our neighborhood and teach penmanship, at a time in America when it was considered an accomplishment to have a "fine hand." His love of transferring words to paper with pen and ink led me straight to my 30-year study of Japanese calligraphy with a *sensei* (master, literally "you who were born before me"). Pursuing this art is a discipline that teaches one to be diligent, not to search for an illusory "perfection," but rather to endeavor to do one's best. And so I say to you, *yoku gambarimashita. You really did your best.*

My favorite saying in Japanese is in a calligraphy I did that hangs on the wall in our living room:

Ichi go ichi e. Treasure this moment, it will never come again.

Wherever your life takes you after the White House, I hope every moment will be treasured.

She Loves Herself When She Is Laughing: Michelle Obama, Taking Down a Stereotype and Co-Creating a Presidency

REBECCA CARROLL

The minute Michelle Obama rolled up to the podium at the 2008 Democratic National Convention wearing that cool mint-green dress, hair laid to the gods, demonstrating what would become her trademark unflinching poise and ineffable ease, it was quite clear that she did not come to play. And some months later, as televised footage of the inauguration of President Barack Obama captures instances when Obama appears more taken with his wife than with the fact that he has just become the country's first Black president, her magnific influence and his gratitude for it is all but palpable.

Michelle Obama is everything a Black man raised by a white single mother in Hawaii needed. She is everything a country with an utterly disgraceful history of emotional and physical violence against Black women should champion and elevate. And I would argue that she represents at least 60 percent of what America will miss most about the Obama presidency.

It would be easy here, and a thousand other times over the past eight years, to trot out the "behind every great man is a great woman" trope, or the "strong Black woman" and "Black superwoman" stereotypes. In truth, though, what Michelle Obama did as First Lady of the United States was take the strong Black woman stereotype and laugh, then kick its ass and tell it to move on out of her way. You see, as she and the President like to say, Michelle Obama has no use for stereotypes or tropes — because they stunt intellectual growth, leave no room for imagination, and are antithetical to the power of hard work, individual strength and self-determination. And if FLOTUS and the President are about anything, it's about the platform of self-determination.

As indomitable as she is today, as a young girl, like most girls and perhaps in particular most young black girls, Michelle did not always lead with confidence. She has admitted to feeling "tangled up in fears and doubts that were entirely of my own creation" when she was a student in high school, and spending too much time worried about her hair and her looks, and what other kids might be saying about her. She has mentioned teachers who openly underestimated her intelligence and prospects to succeed. The beauty, though, of having created her own fears and doubts, is the way in which she has effectively, even casually, decimated them along her path to Princeton, then Harvard Law School, as a successful corporate lawyer, and as a prominent badass in the public sector.

Self-determination is not a mysterious thing — but Michelle makes it seem like it is. For a kid who grew up on the South Side of Chicago with a big brother to trail behind and working-class parents to make proud for their sacrifices, her will and character and complete lack of cynicism are woven throughout her life like threads of magical realism. We can all imagine little girl Michelle in school, working hard and being brave, as the notion evokes almost on cue images of Ruby Bridges and Charlayne Hunter-Gault, alone in the white world of newly integrated schools. But it gets harder to envision when you think about young woman Michelle at Princeton and Harvard in the 1980s — set in between the Black Is Beautiful 70s and the Living Single era of the 90s. Somewhere along the line, she walked into the light and got the hell over.

I marvel at the thought of how my own little brown self would have been influenced growing up with Michelle Obama in the White House. The little brown me, adopted into a white family, surrounded by anti-reflections, inundated by unremitting standards of white beauty, acceptance, worth. Exoticized for my caramel skin and praised for my talents as a dancer and a storyteller early on, when I hit fifth grade, it was as if my skin had somehow suddenly taken on a darker hue — scorched for flying too close to freedom. I wore an afro and sometimes handkerchiefs around my head leaving just a lion's mane ring around my face. I smiled and smiled and laughed and wrote stories and played with friends and felt free. I was free. Until I was not. My fifth-grade teacher, who was mean anyway, made sure to let me know that I was less than all the others — lucky, but in a defying nature sort of way: "very pretty . . . for a black girl. Most black girls aren't very pretty." And with that, I turned inward and lost a faith in my blackness that I never even knew I had until it turned into pride years later.

In middle school I delighted and felt special, somehow redeemed, when one of the most popular boys bought me for the school's annual "Slave Day" — a tradition since quietly phased out, but back then at my regional middle school in rural New England it was a highly anticipated barometer of popularity. Boys would bid on girls, and girls would bid on boys with fake money, even though all the most popular kids were wealthy. The slave you purchased belonged to you as property for an entire day, and you could make them wear and do whatever you wanted. The boy who bought me was, at 12 years old, a competitive ski racer. He dressed me in his tightest fitting racing suit, and I had to wear his heavy ski boots and tinted goggles too.

No one — not teachers, students, librarians, secretaries or the principal — in the entire school gave a second thought to the racial implications of this time-honored tradition. Not a single parent, including my own, mounted a complaint or expressed concern that dedicating a whole day to the buying and selling of people and calling them slaves might be problematic, demeaning or racist. Because in a historical context, I was the sole student who would suffer this impact. There were no other black students. And in fact, I did not exist to anyone in that school until I was purchased property. I reveled in my status as purchase-worthy, while also mindful of how lucky I was to not have the misfortune of looking like most black girls.

A few years later, the boy who bought me was the same boy who asked me to the sophomore prom "as a friend" and who was forbidden by his father to take me, a black girl, because: "You don't want to look back at pictures and see that you took a black girl to the prom."

I'm quite sure that my fifth-grade teacher would have been less kind to little Michelle, with her dark brown skin and full lips. But I also believe that Michelle would not have internalized the comment as I did for years — indeed, could not have internalized the comment and gone on to become who she is and withstand the public scrutiny she has been subjected to since day one.

Even in the late days of the first campaign trail when the media attacked her mercilessly with coded language regarding her toughness and harsh tone and general outspokenness, then and still eight years later, she has never once lost her composure. In fact, she has consistently boosted it up a notch.

Whether demanding to be "greeted properly" with a fist bump while guesting on *The*

View after being ridiculed for the gesture, riffing on the double entendre of "turn up"/turnip, spitting Missy Elliot lyrics, dancing to "Uptown Funk" with the cast from *You Think You Can Dance,* practicing Tai Chi with high school students in China, throwing shade or mitigating straight inappropriate behavior by public figures, shimmying with Jimmy Fallon, rapping about college or flexing her freakishly beautiful, sculpted arms — Michelle Obama's sense of self is distinctly rooted in humor, tenacity and resolute blackness. She is the embodiment of what black American writer Zora Neale Hurston meant when she wrote: "I love myself when I am laughing, and then again when I am looking mean and impressive."

That Hurston quote, which also became the title of the Zora Neale Hurston Reader edited by Alice Walker and published in 1979, comes from Hurston's response to a series of photos taken of her by white photographer and patron of the Harlem Renaissance Carl Van Vechten. Condemned for her independence as an assertive Black woman in the 1930s, Hurston was, if nothing else — and indeed, she was many things — herself. That is no small thing for a Black woman in the 1930s, and sadly, it is no small thing for a Black woman in the 2000s either. But that is, I think, what befuddles and pleases and intoxicates America about Michelle Obama. It doesn't occur to her to be anything other than herself.

She is a civil disrupter with a radical kind of benevolence. She is focused and silly, compelling and humble. It would all be an act if it wasn't. And while some might argue that this is precisely what politicians do and who they are — polished, well prepared, articulate, unflappable — Michelle Obama is not so much a politician as she is a manifestor; the hyper spectacular incarnation of a Black woman unbound. The Black woman who knew when and where she entered on her own terms, evocative of still yet another Hurston quote: "Sometimes, I feel discriminated against, but it does not make me angry. It merely astonishes me. How can any deny themselves the pleasure of my company? It's beyond me."

Whereas these words might be interpreted as a reflection of the Hurston described by many of her critics as contrary and immodest, to me they register as Hurston's manifesto and Obama's preamble. Michelle Obama would never speak such words, but she doesn't need to — they rest high in her taut brown shoulders, gather in meaning as her hands gesture in that trademark make-it-plain way, march quietly in the crescent of her broad, knowing smile, and are released in the sureness of her stride.

Among the most remarked upon attributes of Zora Neale Hurston is how centered she was in her Blackness, and how racially ambiguous she appeared. Light-skinned, and likely identified by the term at the top of her own personally created color scale — "high yaller" — she could have easily passed for white in various circles, and yet, she didn't, couldn't, wasn't about that. She was ardently committed to her culture and kinfolk, and her place among them. There is no mistaking Michelle Obama for anything but Black — although one gets the clear impression that she would evince the same cultural devotion if she looked anything like Hurston.

And that — the full immersion, gratitude and integrity regarding her Blackness and that of those she loves — is perhaps the most appreciable reason that Barack chose her. I might be less inclined to be so bold in my presumption about why the President of the United States loves his wife, if not for the deep well of empathy I have for the younger Barack Obama — the Barack in *Dreams from My Father: A Story of Race and Inheritance,* who writes: "Away from my mother, away from my grandparents, I was engaged in a fitful interior struggle. I was trying to raise myself to be a Black man in America, and beyond the given of my appearance, no one around me seemed to know exactly what that meant." Michelle Obama knew what that meant.

As a Black adoptee growing up in a white family, it also fell upon me to raise myself to be Black whilst no one around me had any idea what that meant — but I was sure as hell going to find a partner who did — whenever or if ever it came time to get married, or to settle in with someone for the duration. About this intention, I wrote some years ago: "I was going to marry a Black man. That was the mandate. He would validate my own Blackness, and allow me to reemerge as the Black woman I always knew I was but wasn't able to express. I would happily, freely shed any and all remnants of an identity shaped by being raised in a white family, attending all-white schools, and the imbued notion that I would be a better and more appealing person, friend, girlfriend, if I were white."

It didn't end up that way for me, because ultimately, you love who you love. And as it turns out, if you are Black, who you marry doesn't make you any less or more so. But I understand well, and recognize duly that Barack Obama could not deny himself the company of a woman who loves herself and her Blackness when she is laughing, and then again when she's looking mean and impressive.

THE BEST OF WIVES AND BEST OF WOMEN

PHILLIPA SOO

Before *Hamilton* moved to Broadway, we were at the Public Theater in New York. After the opening number, "Alexander Hamilton," I had a crossover. I had to go down the stairs and I had to change and then I had to cross over and come back up. One day while crossing over, I opened the door to the backstage stairwell space, and there was a very tall man in a suit, with one of those earpieces. It was the Secret Service. I was like, "Oh. Please be careful. Sorry, I don't mean to run into you." I was like, "I think there's going to be people coming in and out. I got to go, bye." It was such a quick, awkward exchange but I thought, *Somebody is here. Somebody's here today who's very important.* We had had some celebrities coming to the show, I assumed it was a politician, but I didn't know who.

I had anticipated that the First Lady might come, one day, when we made it to Broadway, but downtown — at the Public Theater? It wasn't until after the show ended that they said, "Michelle Obama's here!" At the time I shared a dressing room with Jasmine Cephas Jones and Reneé Elise Goldsberry, my Schuyler sisters. We hurriedly got out of costume to say hello. Giddy with excitement, we made our way to the greenroom. There she stood. So poised and beautiful. She said hello to each and every one of us. I will never forget what Mrs. Obama said, "This is the best piece of art that I've ever seen." I was floored. She has seen so much art in her life. Coming from her, our First Lady, the modern-day Schuyler sister incarnate, and one of the most inspirational women of our time, it was the best compliment I have ever received.

Hamilton is, of course, closely tied to the Obamas because Lin first performed the opening number at a White House poetry jam. I didn't know anything about Eliza when I first got the call about *Hamilton*. Tommy Kail, the director, asked me if I wanted to be a part of it. I knew what he was talking about because I'd seen the video of Lin performing it at the White House for Barack and Michelle Obama. I specifically remember a friend showing me that YouTube clip while I was a student in drama school. Cut to five or six years later when Tommy calls me and asks me to be a part of a December reading of Act II of what was then called "Hamilton Mixtape." I did what most people do when they don't know something, I googled Eliza. I saw that she was his wife but there wasn't a lot more. I just chalked it up to me being a lazy researcher. I thought, *Okay. I'll do digging later. I'll go and see what this project is and enjoy the experience.* Hearing the music for the first time was incredible. It had such an instant cool factor. But it wasn't until I got into the room with Lin, Alex, and Tommy (I would end up working with Andy a few months later) that I truly discovered what the "Hamilton Mixtape" really was. I thought: *These artists and creators that I'm working with . . . this story . . . is going to change the world. And I get to be in this room.* And it changed me, too. I just didn't know it yet.

In December of 2013, the end of the play still hadn't been written. It actually wasn't until that workshop in January, a day before our presentation, that Lin gave me the last song. In the moment at the end of *Hamilton* when Eliza steps out and you see her, most people tell me they are so taken aback. "Oh my gosh! *She's* the one who is telling us this story, like we're learning this story because of *her.*" That was the way that I felt getting that last song. A moment of: *Really? And you want me to finish the play? I mean I'd love to but . . .*

Lin went on to explain that in the song you look and see everything that she did after Hamilton died. I was just as surprised and awestruck by the beauty of this woman's legacy that not many people know about, and how beautiful this moment was that we're giving her, a voice and a place in history for the first time. It's huge.

My grandmother was a classical pianist so I grew up with Schubert, Mozart, Beethoven. I studied piano as a kid. My musical background and upbringing was very much a mix. Right out of school I did this show called *Natasha, Pierre & the Great Comet of 1812.* It is based on a classical text with new music — not necessarily confined by a certain genre. It was a diverse, interesting group of musicians, actors, nonactors and singers all creating this thing that is bigger than all of us. We couldn't have done it on our own; we had to come together in this particular way to make it. I feel like that led me to *Hamilton* because they are very similar in that way, both based on a moment in history.

Singing *Hamilton* each night feels like such a release. It's so brilliantly written and the style of each song is so specifically chosen for the character and what they're going through. Developing the show became like a fun game of "How can I make everything that I'm looking at on this page and everything I'm hearing inform me as an actor about Eliza, and where she is in her life, and what she might be feeling?" It's kind of like playing detective. It's like when you are reading Shakespeare, a very similar experience. You're looking at the text — the structure, the poetic imagery, the rhythm — to inform you of what's happening in the scene. It was fun.

When Eliza says, "I took myself out of the narrative," in reference to guarding her privacy after Hamilton's cheating is revealed, her situation feels stunningly contemporary. It took me a while to understand this particular moment in Eliza's journey. In discovering how to play Eliza, I first asked myself, "What is the difference between the common woman then and the common woman now?" But that proved to be less useful. I was only separating myself from Eliza. So I started to ask the question,

"What do all women, past and present have in common?" The answer: survival. Women have struggled a great deal, yes. But it has been their ability to overcome, the way women have chosen to deal with their struggles. Not only survive, but flourish through their achievements. The struggle is real, the struggle has always been real and will continue to be real. It's just a matter of *how* you choose to find your way through whatever challenges you face. Eliza is empowered by taking herself out of the narrative. I think that's why forgiveness is such a huge part of the play.

People seem confused when Eliza forgives Hamilton. I suppose it is because we have more options now. It's easy to opt to avoid someone, avoid forgiveness, avoid conflict, or avoid complicated feelings, love and disgust, that coexist. But ultimately it doesn't matter how many options we have; it is a miracle that we choose to survive.

One of the amazing things about *Hamilton* is the way it makes us feel less distant from the people we know to be our Founding Fathers and Founding Mothers. A few weeks ago, we all went to the White House to perform the musical and to work with students as part of the educational initiative around *Hamilton.* I could tell just from watching Mrs. Obama that she has such an awareness of what it means to bring people together, how important that is. We can all be doing our separate thing amazingly, but when you bring groups together the way she does, it can actually create something better than you could have imagined.

I truly believe that the energy that I experienced that day at the White House was because of how the Obamas like to run their workspace, how they like to have people greeted and feel like they are a part of the White House, even if it's your first time there. It was just very exemplary of the idea of, What is your profession? What is your calling? and then, What is your role as a citizen? And how do those two things go together? How do they inform each other and when can you do them at the same time? The notion of artist as citizen is at the very heart of *Hamilton.* For me, growing up half Chinese, I feel very American for the first time in my life and I feel very much like who I am as a citizen is right in the same car as who I am as an artist, which doesn't always happen. That's a really beautiful thing and I hope that the rest of my work can be artist-to-citizen inspired.

The Obamas have shaped my journey as an adult in a profound way. I remember being in New York when they were elected. I remember being in Times Square. I remember hearing cheers in the streets. I remember just being so excited. It's kind of funny. My journey from Chicago to New York runs on a parallel timeline of their journey from Chicago to the White House.

I visited D.C. on a school trip, as a teenager. At the time, my biggest concern was "Am I going to get a CIA hat or an FBI hat?" But there's something about *Hamilton* and what it's doing to young people that's making history and the intricacies of who governs and how we govern come alive. *Hamilton* reminds us that the Founding Fathers and Founding Mothers were real people.

I went back to visit my cousin who goes to school in D.C. in November of '14 right before we started rehearsals. It was research, but also to see her. We went to the museums, we went to the monuments, and I remember thinking, *This place I experienced before is very different than what I'm experiencing now.* I feel like I am tied to this place somehow, whereas I didn't before. I think eighth graders going to D.C. now have a totally different outlook on the trip because of *Hamilton*.

The show has made me feel more American in the way that I am interested in being involved in how we live and continue to live. It has made me realize that I do have a voice and that the power does not reside in the beings that are the higher-ups. It starts with us, it starts from the ground up, which is how this nation was built. I think the second time that Barack Obama came to see *Hamilton,* when he brought the Democratic National Committee, that was very much what he was addressing. We can't forget, with all of these issues that we're trying to address, that so much of the change starts with us in this room, with conversation, with ideas, with curiosity, with questions.

In his last letter to Eliza, Hamilton calls her "the best of wives and the best of women." If I'm trying to get into Hamilton's brain, he was saying "best of wives" like "best of who you are to me" and "best of women," meaning who you are to the world. The letter used to be in the show. I used to read it. I still remember every line:

This letter, my very dear Eliza, will not be delivered to you, unless I shall first have terminated my earthly career to begin, as I humbly hope from redeeming grace and divine mercy, a happy immortality.

If it had been possible for me to have

avoided the interview, my love for you and my precious children would have been alone a decisive motive. But it was not possible, without sacrifices which would have rendered me unworthy of your esteem. I need not tell you of the pangs I feel, from the idea of quitting you and exposing you to the anguish which I know you would feel. Nor could I dwell on the topic lest it should un-man me.

The consolations of Religion, my be-loved, can alone support you and these you have a right to enjoy. Fly to the bosom of your God and be comforted. With my last idea I shall cherish the sweet hope of meeting you in a better world.

Adieu best of wives and best of Women. Embrace all my darling Chil-dren for me.

Ever yours

I used to read it, and I don't anymore. I think we cut it out for time's sake, but the idea of the letter still lives. It's chilling. It gives me chills.

I'm a total believer in the universe and the over soul. Somehow the energy that our

Founding Mothers put into our history has lasted and has traversed centuries and found its way to me. Eventually, it will leave me and find its way to somebody else. It does feel like ages have passed by the end of the three-hour play so I definitely use that. Because *Hamilton* has had such a universal voice, it's brought some of the most amazing women into my life. Women who are politicians, who are actors, who are writers, who are my family members that I respect so much, strangers — mothers and daughters who have lost their loved ones, all of these women, choosing to survive. And to be able to share it with them in this way, I feel like it's paying homage to them, it's paying homage to Eliza, and to all the other versions of Eliza that have existed throughout history and will exist for ages to come.

Making Space

ROXANE GAY

As President Barack Obama's second term winds down, we are in the middle of a contentious and unbelievable election season. As we look forward, this is also a good time to consider Obama's legacy — the good and bad of what he has accomplished over the past eight years and, of course, what it means for Barack Hussein Obama to have been the first black president of the United States. His two-term presidency has offered a lot to consider and critique, to appreciate and admire.

As a black woman, I am considering not only the president's legacy, but that of his wife, Michelle Obama — lawyer, wife, mother, and the first African American First Lady — as much a pioneer in her role as her husband in his because she made space for black womanhood in unprecedented ways.

When you really think about it, the role of

First Lady is decidedly unenviable, particularly when considering the role from a feminist perspective. For four to eight years, a woman becomes a professional spouse. Her identity is irrevocably wrapped up in her husband's political ambitions and position before, during, and after the presidency. The First Lady is judged for how well she comports herself as a professional wife and a professional woman where the version of womanhood to which she must conform is highly constrained. It would be very easy for a woman to lose herself in such circumstances — smiling by her husband's side at state dinners, choosing state china, doing socially acceptable "good works" without appearing to have political ambitions of her own, regardless of her accomplishments before stepping into the role.

The role of First Lady is not without its perks. The First Lady has, typically, been afforded a modicum of benevolence from the press and the American public. She has, in many cases, served as a fashion icon, and been allowed to humanize the deeply political institution of the presidency. Such has not been the case for Michelle Obama. As the first black woman to fill the role of First Lady, Michelle Obama's position has been even more unenviable. Since President

215

Obama ran for his first term in office, Michelle Obama has faced a level of scrutiny, criticism, and insult that is unprecedented. She has rarely been treated like an icon but despite the obstacles she has faced, Michelle Obama has risen to the occasion and exceeded all expectations of a First Lady.

In an article for *More* magazine, during the 2008 campaign, Geraldine Brooks wrote of Michelle Obama, "The very qualities that make her an icon of 21st-century womanhood — her strong opinions, her frankness in expressing them, the confidence born of bootstrap triumphs — make her a rich target for those who still believe that outspoken woman and first lady should never be synonymous." Brooks is correct, but she overlooks how blackness also made Michelle Obama a target. Over the past nine or ten years, she has not only been attacked for being outspoken. Her femininity, demeanor, and suitability for the role of First Lady have also been questioned and derided largely because of her race and unapologetic pride in her blackness, her womanhood, her Chicago roots, her intelligence and education, and her humanity.

Despite the obstacles she has faced, Michelle Obama has taken to the unenviable role of First Lady with grace, verve, and intelligence. Given her many accomplishments prior to 2008, this is no surprise, but it has been a real pleasure to see a woman who knows what it is like to live in this world in a black woman's body, in the White House, reinventing the role of First Lady and making space for black girls and women to believe that we too can rise, rise, rise.

It has been a real pleasure to watch Michelle Obama gleefully defying those who try to diminish her. Over the past two terms, I have admired Michelle Obama's frankness and her refusal to place her husband on a pedestal. He may well be president but he is also the man she married, flawed and human. She is unapologetically committed to her family, going so far as to have her mother, Marian Robinson, live in the White House with the Obama family, so as to help the First Daughters, Sasha and Malia, have some semblance of a normal life.

I am even more admiring of the work she has done — initiatives to combat obesity, particularly among children, working with military families, advocating for women and especially black girls and black women. She has supported Barack Obama's policies and, to my mind, pushed him to be more progressive. She has traveled the world over and spoken her mind, representing herself, the First Family, the United States. Michelle Obama has been carefree enough to do "Carpool Karaoke" with late-night host James Corden. She has been a style icon with amazing musculature and flawless hair. Whenever I think about Michelle Obama, I think, "When I grow up, I want to be just like her." I want to be that intelligent, confident, and comfortable in my own skin.

As she represents the United States, Michelle Obama is clear-eyed about this country and what it means to be a black woman living in a black body, in this country. During her speech at the 2016 Democratic National Convention, she said, "I wake up every morning in a house that was built by slaves." It was a stunning moment, a stunning reminder that no matter how high you rise in the United States, there is a history to which you are tethered.

It is a bitter, terrible thing, to live in the most recognizable and powerful house in the country, if not the world, and to be surrounded by such a constant, intimate reminder of a disgraceful institution with which the United States has yet to fully reckon. And yet, Michelle Obama faces that reminder with steely grace. She is vocal in reminding the American people, if not the world, that we cannot nor should not forget the sins of slavery. She makes space for difficult but necessary conversations about race and how we must reckon with race.

What thrills me most about Michelle Obama is that the full extent of her legacy is yet to be written. As fiercely as she has served in the role of First Lady, she has been constrained by political realities and the expectations of the role, of the whole world. When Obama leaves office in January 2017, those constraints will be gone and many incredible opportunities will be available to her.

I hope Michelle Obama does whatever her heart most desires when her husband's presidency ends, but I would love to see her make space for black girls and women in the public sphere and the public imagination. In a perfect world, she might create and lead a robust and well-funded organization dedicated to black girls and women, one that implements a set of initiatives that encourage black girls and women to flourish.

There is precedent. In 2014, the Obama administration created the My Brother's Keeper program to support young black men, focusing on six key issues — preparing children to enter school, ensuring that children are reading at grade level by the third grade, educating children so that when they graduate high school they are ready to either continue on to college or embark on a career, creating opportunities for people to finish college education or professional training, preparing people to participate fully in the workforce, and making sure that children are safe from violence and, should they make mistakes, be able to take advantage of second chances.

The program has met with both praise and criticism, and one of the most significant criticisms has been that My Brother's Keeper is designed specifically for black boys and men. While this demographic does need such a program, black girls and women are equally vulnerable, but often overlooked. When we talk about blackness, all too often black women are ignored, whether discussing police violence, education, professional opportunities, or personal success. Black women are the footnotes to the dominant discourse about blackness. Worse yet, black women are all too often beholden to the trope of the "strong black woman," able to be all things and do all things, while asking for nothing in return.

Like My Brother's Keeper, I would love to see a program that focuses on the importance of education and ensuring that young girls and women and their families or support networks are adequately prepared to fully participate in our education system. I want this program to help black women enter and succeed in the workforce. I want this program to help black girls and women from all walks of life, with a particular focus on supporting women who have been incarcerated. I want this program to support black women dealing with not only state violence but domestic and sexual violence.

I also want a program that offers black girls and women support and education for their physical and emotional well-being. Contemporary blackness takes a toll. In an article for *The New York Times,* "Black Health Matters," Jenna Wortham discussed the stress of absorbing the recent murders of Philando Castile and Alton Sterling. She wrote that such tragedies, "force you to reconcile your own helplessness in the face of such brutal injustice, and the terrifying reality that it could happen to you, or someone you hold dear." Wortham went on to say that, "Making space to deal with the psychological toll of racism is absolutely necessary." Not enough black women make that kind of space and this society certainly doesn't make that kind of space.

Most social initiatives focus on the material — education, employment, safety — while overlooking the emotional. Michelle Obama is uniquely qualified to lead a movement that considers the entirety of a woman's well-being — mind, body, and soul.

Michelle Obama was the first African American First Lady of the United States. Her future is full of possibilities, and though she has already gone above and beyond in her service to this country, I hope she still has a will to serve beyond the White House. A woman with Michelle Obama's intelligence, background, strength of will, and cultural prominence is well positioned to lead an initiative that helps black women and girls to live in a country built by slaves and still burdened by slavery's legacy, that helps black women and girls to thrive in a culture that seeks to demean and diminish them at every turn. She has made space for herself in inhospitable spaces, throughout her career. With this organization, she could continue that work so that more black girls and women learn how to make and hold space for themselves in this world.

CONTRIBUTOR BIOGRAPHIES

Veronica Chambers is currently a John S. Knight fellow at Stanford University. She's a prolific author, best known for her critically acclaimed memoir *Mama's Girl* and the award-winning memoir *Yes Chef,* which was co-authored with chef Marcus Samuelsson. She has collaborated on four *New York Times* bestsellers, most recently *32 Yolks,* which she co-wrote with chef Eric Ripert. *The New Yorker* called *Mama's Girl* "a troubling testament to grit and mother love . . . one of the finest and most evenhanded in the genre." *Mama's Girl* has been course-adopted by hundreds of high schools and colleges. Born in Panama and raised in Brooklyn, she writes often about her Afro-Latina heritage. She lives with her husband and daughter in northern California. You can connect with her on Twitter @vvchambers.

Nominated for two Academy Awards and four Golden Globes, writer/director **Ava Duvernay's** most recent feature *Selma* was one of 2015's most critically acclaimed films. She is currently writing, directing and producing her first television series, *Queen Sugar,* for Oprah Winfrey's OWN. Winner of the 2012 Sundance Film Festival's Best Director Prize for her previous feature *Middle of Nowhere,* DuVernay's earlier directorial work includes *I Will Follow, Venus Vs, My Mic Sounds Nice* and *This is The Life.* She founded ARRAY, a distribution collective for filmmakers of color and women, in 2010, and was named one of Fast Company's Most Innovative Companies in Hollywood 2016. DuVernay was born and raised in Los Angeles, California.

Benilde Little is the bestselling author of the novels *Good Hair, The Itch, Acting Out, Who Does She Think She Is?* and *Welcome to My Breakdown.* She has been featured in *The New York Times, The Washington Post, Essence, Jet, People Magazine, Heart and Soul* and *MORE,* among many others as well as on NPR, the *Today Show* and the *Tavis Smiley* show. The national book club, the Go On Girls, selected *Good Hair* as the best novel of the year. Natalie Cole bought the film rights. Benilde's writing has appeared in numerous anthologies, including *Honey, Hush!* and *About Face.* She was a finalist for an NAACP Image Award. A former reporter for *The Cleveland Plain Dealer, The Star Ledger* and *People* magazine, she was also a senior editor at *Essence.* She has been a creative writing professor at Ramapo College and now teaches writing at The Writers Circle. She graduated from Howard University and attended graduate school at Northwestern. She and her husband live in Montclair, New Jersey, with their teenage son, Ford. Their daughter, Baldwin, is away at college.

Damon Young is the editor-in-chief of VSB. He is also a contributing editor for EBONY.com. And a columnist for *EBONY* magazine. And a founding editor for *1839.* Damon is busy. He lives in Pittsburgh, and he really likes pancakes. Reach him at damon@verysmartbrothas.com. Or don't.

With signature style, humor and irreverence, **Alicia Hall Moran's** style combines the world of Broadway (starring as "Bess" on the 9-month National Tour of the Tony-winning production), the world of visual art (her musical work can currently be seen in the 56th Venice Biennale) and the languages of classical music and jazz.

Since 2010, Ms. Moran's critically acclaimed chamber music soul revue, Alicia Hall Moran + the motown project, has been thrilling audiences at The Highline Ballroom, (Le) Poisson Rouge, as well as at universities across America. Ms. Moran upholds the traditions of her great-great-uncle Hall Johnson (legendary choral director, composer and preserver of the Negro Spiritual) and her greatest teachers (Shirley Verrett, Adele Addison, Hilda Harris, David Jones and Warren Wilson) while exploring new ways to celebrate the repertoire of the classics and the genius of American song.

Jazz pianist, composer and performance artist **Jason Moran** was born in Houston, Texas, in 1975 and earned a degree from the Manhattan School of Music, where he studied with Jaki Byard. He was named a MacArthur Fellow in 2010 and is the Artistic Director for Jazz at The Kennedy Center. Moran currently teaches at the New England Conservatory of Music in Boston, Massachusetts.

Moran's rich and varied body of work is actively shaping the current and future landscape of jazz. He has collaborated with such major figures as Adrian Piper, Joan Jonas, Glenn Ligon, Stan Douglas, Adam Pendleton, Lorna Simpson, and Kara Walker; commissioning institutions of Moran's work include the Walker Art Center, the Philadelphia Museum of Art, the Dia Art Foundation, the Whitney Museum of American Art, Jazz at Lincoln Center and Harlem Stage.

Moran has a long-standing collaborative practice with his wife, the singer and Broadway actress Alicia Hall Moran; as named artists in the 2012 Whitney Biennial, they together constructed BLEED, a five-day series of live music.

Moran will have his first solo museum exhibition at the Walker Art Center, Minneapolis, Minnesota, in spring 2018.

Brittney Cooper is Assistant Professor of Women's and Gender Studies and Africana Studies at Rutgers University. A Black feminist theorist, she specializes in the study of Black women's intellectual history, Hip Hop generation feminism, and race and gender representation in popular culture. Her forthcoming book, *Race Women: Gender and the Making of a Black Public Intellectual Tradition,* examines the long history of Black women's thought leadership in the U.S., with a view toward reinvigorating contemporary scholarly and popular conversations about Black feminism.

Dr. Cooper is also a sought-after public speaker and commentator. In addition to a weekly column on race and gender politics at Salon.com, her work and words have appeared in *The New York Times, The Washington Post,* Cosmo.com, TV Guide, the *Los Angeles Times,* Ebony.com, The Root.com, MSNBC's *Melissa Harris-Perry Show, All In With Chris Hayes, Disrupt with Karen Finney* and *Third Rail* on Al-Jazeera America, among many others. She is also a cofounder of the Crunk Feminist Collective, a popular feminist blog. Dr. Brittney Cooper is a proud alumna of Howard University (class of 2002) and proud native of North Louisiana.

Ylonda Gault Caviness is author of the parenting memoir *Child, Please* and a *New York Times* Op-Ed contributor. An award-winning journalist, she has specialized in issues related to child advocacy, family and motherhood for more than a decade. Gault's work has appeared in *Essence, The New York Times, Redbook* and Salon.com. She is a single mom of three awesome children.

Chirlane McCray is the First Lady of New York City, a writer and a passionate advocate for the underserved.

Ms. McCray is the driving force behind ThriveNYC, the most comprehensive mental health plan of any city or state in the USA. ThriveNYC is changing the culture around mental health and substance misuse, reimagining the way government and its partners deliver services and making it easier for people to get help in the places where they live, work, worship, and learn.

The First Lady is honored to serve as Chair of the Mayor's Fund to Advance New York City. The Mayor's Fund is the City's official nonprofit — a one-of-a-kind organization that brings together government, philanthropies and the private sector to work on some of the most pressing issues of our time, including mental health, youth workforce development and immigration and citizenship. She is also Honorary Co-Chair of the Commission on Gender Equity, and is guiding efforts to create a city where every girl and woman is treated equally and feels safe.

Ms. McCray and Mayor Bill de Blasio have two remarkable children, Chiara and

Dante. You can learn more about the First Lady's work on Facebook, Twitter, Instagram and Tumblr. She invites New Yorkers to help her make the greatest city in the world even greater.

Cathi Hanauer is the author of three novels, *Gone, Sweet Ruin* and *My Sister's Bones* and the editor of the #10 *New York Times* bestselling essay collection *The Bitch in the House: 26 Women Tell the Truth about Sex, Solitude, Work, Motherhood and Marriage,* which was called out in Deborah Felder's *A Bookshelf of Our Own: Must-Reads for Women.* She has written articles, essays and/or reviews for *The New York Times, Elle, O, Self, Glamour, Whole Living, Mademoiselle, Parenting, Child, Redbook* and other magazines; she was the monthly books columnist for both *Glamour* and *Mademoiselle* and wrote the monthly advice column *Relating* in *Seventeen* for seven years. She has taught writing at The New School, in New York, and at the University of Arizona, in Tucson, as well as privately. She lives in Northampton, Massachusetts, with her husband, writer and *New York Times Modern Love* editor Daniel Jones, and their daughter and son.

Named to Fast Company's League of Extraordinary Women, **Tiffany Dufu** was a Launch Team member to Lean In and is Chief Leadership Officer to Levo, the fastest-growing millennial professional network. She is a consultant to Fortune 500 companies, a sought-after speaker on women's leadership and has presented at Fortune's Most Powerful Women Summit, MAKERS and TEDWomen. She earned a BA and MA in English from the University of Washington. She is the author of *Drop the Ball: Achieving More by Doing Less.*

Tanisha C. Ford is Associate Professor of Black American Studies and History at the University of Delaware. She is the author of *Liberated Threads: Black Women, Style, and the Global Politics of Soul,* which narrates the powerful intertwining histories of the Black Freedom movement and the rise of the global fashion industry. *Liberated Threads* won the 2016 Organization of American Historians' Liberty Legacy Foundation Award for best book on civil rights history. Ford is an expert on social movement history, feminist issues, material culture and fashion, beauty and body politics. Her public writing and cultural commentary has been featured in diverse media

231

outlets and publications including *The New York Times, The Root, The New Yorker, Ebony,* NPR's *Code Switch, Fusion, News One, New York* magazine's *The Cut, Yahoo! Style, Vibe Vixen, Feministing, The Journal of Southern History, NKA: Journal of Contemporary African Art, The Black Scholar* and New York City's HOT 97.

Marcus Samuelsson is an internationally acclaimed chef who has thrilled the food scene with a blend of culture and artistic excellence. Marcus caught the attention of the culinary world at Aquavit. During his tenure as executive chef, he received an impressive three-star rating from *The New York Times,* the youngest person ever to receive such an accolade.

In addition to being a successful cookbook author, Marcus released his *New York Times* bestselling and James Beard–winning memoir *Yes, Chef* in 2012 to rave reviews. In 2009, Marcus was honored as a guest chef at the White House under the Obama administration, where he planned and executed the administration's first state dinner for the first family, Prime Minister Singh of India and 400 of their guests. He has been a UNICEF ambassador since

2000, focusing his advocacy on water and sanitation issues, specifically the Tap Project. Marcus also had the honor of speaking at the 2011 Annual Meeting of the World Economic Forum in Davos, Switzerland, and TEDxHarlem in 2012.

His iconic Red Rooster Harlem celebrates the roots of American cuisine in one of New York City's liveliest and most culturally rich neighborhoods. It has earned two stars from *The New York Times* and countless accolades for its food, style and connection to the community.

Sarah Lewis received her bachelor's degree from Harvard, an M. Phil from Oxford University, and her Ph.D. from Yale University in the History of Art. Lewis's research interests focus on representations of race in contemporary art and nineteenth- and early-twentieth-century American culture and across the Black Atlantic world and the Black Sea region. Her scholarship has been published in many academic journals as well as in *The New Yorker, The New York Times, Artforum, Art in America* and in publications for the Smithsonian, The Museum of Modern Art and Rizzoli. Lewis is also the author of *The Rise: Creativity, the Gift of Failure, and the Search for Mastery,* which has been translated into six languages.

Lewis has served on President Obama's Arts Policy Committee and currently serves on the advisory council of the *International Review of African-American Art* and the board of the Andy Warhol Foundation of the Visual Arts, Creative Time and The CUNY Graduate Center. Before joining the faculty at Harvard, she held curatorial positions at The Museum of Modern Art, New York, and the Tate Modern, London, and taught at Yale University School of Art. She lives in Cambridge, Massachusetts, and New York City.

Karen Hill Anton is the author of *Crossing Cultures,* a collection of her long-running column in the *Japan Times.* The popular column, praised for its sensitive and no-nonsense approach to cross-cultural living, chronicles her unique life experience as an American woman (from Washington Heights) married to an American (from Greenwich Village) living and raising four bilingual children in rural Japan since 1975.

Rebecca Carroll is a producer of special projects on race at WNYC/New York Public Radio, among them the critically acclaimed podcast on gentrification in central Brooklyn, New York, *There Goes the Neighborhood*. She is a regular opinion writer at *The Guardian* US, a critic-at-large for the *Los Angeles Times* and the author of five nonfiction books, including *Saving the Race* and the award-winning *Sugar in the Raw*.

Phillipa Soo received a 2016 Tony nomination for her Broadway debut as Eliza Hamilton in Lin-Manuel Miranda's gargantuan hit, *Hamilton*. She originated the role off-Broadway at the Public Theater. Soo also starred as Natasha in the acclaimed off-Broadway run of the immersive musical *Natasha, Pierre and the Great Comet of 1812*. Her other stage credits include *A Little Night Music* and *School for Wives*.

Roxane Gay's writing appears in *Best American Mystery Stories 2014, Best American Short Stories 2012, Best Sex Writing 2012, A Public Space, McSweeney's, Tin House, Oxford American, American Short Fiction, Virginia Quarterly Review,* and many others. She is a contributing opinion writer for *The New York Times*. She is the author of the books *Ayiti, An Untamed State,* the *New York Times* bestselling *Bad Feminist,* and *Difficult Women* and *Hunger* forthcoming in 2017. She is also the author of *World of Wakanda* for Marvel.

ACKNOWLEDGMENTS

One day, I left my office to have lunch with St. Martin's editor Elisabeth Dyssegaard, whom I have been lucky enough to know for years. By the end of lunch, we were talking about Michelle Obama and Elisabeth shared that she had an idea for a small collection of essays from a surprising mix of contributors that would be both a tribute and an exploration of this ground-breaking and iconic First Lady. This anthology was her brain child and I'm so grateful to her for giving me the opportunity to move from mere Michelle O fandom to the dozens of conversations, meetings, emails, drafts and edits that led to this book. Thank you, Elisabeth.

I've never met Michelle Obama, but the beauty of who she has been these past eight years is that you don't need to know her personally to bask in all that she has offered this country. Thank you, Michelle, for showing a generation of women, including me and my daughter, what it means to dwell in possibility.

I owe a bounty of thanks to the writers who said yes to this project: Benilde Little, Damon Young, Jason Moran, Dr. Brittney Cooper, Dr. Sarah Lewis, Dr. Tanisha Ford, Tiffany Dufu, Karen Hill Anton, Rebecca Carroll, Roxane Gay and Ylonda Gault Caviness. Chirlane McCray offered her unique perspective on Michelle O through the lens of her work as First Lady of New York City. Phillipa Soo took time from her turn on Broadway in *Hamilton* to craft a stunning essay about the artist as citizen. Marcus Samuelsson has been my friend for as long as I can remember. He has artfully used food as a platform for his relentless curiosity about the world and I am always inspired by his vision and unique perspective. It's an honor to have his voice in this collection. Ava DuVernay is the busiest woman in filmmaking and yet, across continents and time zones, she offered not only her words, but her support and encouragement about the importance of this project and for that I am grateful.

Two more contributors deserve special praise. Jason Moran calls Alicia Hall Moran "the Brain" and the title is fitting. Alicia is not only a gifted vocalist. She is someone who, to paraphrase the words of the old Warner Brothers slogan, educates, entertains and enlightens. She is a big thinker and I'm happy to know her. I'm also especially happy that, through this book, you will get to know her a little too.

Cathi Hanauer gave me my first regular writing gig when I was an eighteen-year-old writer at *Seventeen* magazine. That job helped me to quit four of my six work-study jobs and to see myself as a professional writer at such an early age. Then, when I turned thirty, Cathi changed my life again by inviting me to contribute to her trailblazing anthology, *The Bitch in the House: 26 Women Tell the Truth about Sex, Solitude, Work, Motherhood, and Marriage.* Then she invited me back for the sequel, *The Bitch is Back: Older, Wiser, and (Getting) Happier.* Because of this, she is the only friend who gets to call me bitch. I am always appreciative of Cathi's editorial advice and mentorship. But I am especially proud that she took the time to craft the essay in this collection. Cathi, you're amazing and I adore you.

I have contributed to a number of anthologies but never ever knew how much work was involved in putting them together. So I want to say a special thank-you to *Mommy*

Wars editor Leslie Morgan Steiner; *Black Cool* editor Rebecca Walker and *Becoming American* editor Nana-Ama Danquah for all of your hard work, patience and vision.

Caroline Kim is not in this book but she worked tirelessly and generously, as she always does, behind the scenes to make it happen. Cline, if I could put your name on the cover of this book, I would. I'm grateful to the agents and managers who worked with us on this book: the wonderful Faith Childs, Eric Simonoff and his team, Meg Mortimer and Jessica Morgulis, Ashley Bode and Jenn Burka. Thanks too, to Tilane Jones at Array Now. Thanks to the team at St. Martin's: Alan Bradshaw, Laura Apperson, Courtney Reed, Laura Clark, Jennifer Simington and Staci Burt. Leah Kaplan provided invaluable research assistance. I'm also grateful for the conversations about this book that I had with Lynette Clemetson, Dr. Janet Taylor, Katherine Wessling and Lise Funderburg. Neuehouse New York provided a lovely space to work, and I'm grateful to Andy Kahan for making the Free Library of Philadelphia one of my second homes.

Our friends, Mai and Luis Yerovi and their daughters, Maia and Olivia, are a part of our extended family. We're grateful to them for being so close even when the distance between us is great. I am thankful to our family, for their time, experience, guidance and humor: Jerry and Mary Clampet, Cecilia and Antonio Ortega, Diana and Buster Richards. I'm grateful for all Michelle O has modeled for our nieces and play-nieces: Maggie Clampet-Lundquist, Sophia Clampet-Lundquist, Chelsea Clemetson, Cameron Lawrence and Sophie Gono.

Finally, thanks to my home team: Jason Clampet states the facts, Flora Clampet plays the tracks.

NOTES

Michelle in High Cotton

1. *The Daily Beast,* August 21, 2009.
2. Geraldine Brooks, "Michelle Obama and the Roots of Reinvention," *More,* October 2008.
3. Peter McCaffrey, *Michelle Obama: First Lady* (Women of Achievement) (New York: Chelsea House Publishers, 2010), p. 88.
4. Touré, "Black and White on Martha's Vineyard," *New York,* June 29, 2009.
5. Brooks, "Michelle Obama and the Roots of Reinvention."
6. Robin Givham, "Five Myths about Michelle Obama," *Washington Post,* January 10, 2014. Givham was quoting from Michelle Obama's Princeton senior thesis, "Princeton-Educated Blacks and the Black Community," written under her maiden name, Michelle LaVaughn Robin-

son, in 1985.

7. "Remarks by the President and First Lady at College Opportunity Summit," The White House Briefing Room, January 16, 2014, https://www.whitehouse.gov/the-press-office/2014/01/16/remarks-president-and-first-lady-college-opportunity-summit.

8. Carol Felsenthal, "The Making of a First Lady," *Chicago,* February 2009.

9. Ibid.

10. Jodi Kantor and Monica Davey, "Crossed Paths: Chicago's Jacksons and Obamas," *New York Times,* February 24, 2013; Jerome R. Corsi, "Jesse Jackson, Wright 'Arranged' Obama Marriage," WND, October 4, 2012, http://www.wnd.com/2012/10/jesse-jackson-wright-arranged-obama-marriage/.Corsi10/4/2012.

11. Peter Slevin, *Michelle Obama: A Life* (New York: Knopf, 2015), p. 35.

12. Rebecca Johnson, "Michelle Obama: The Natural," *Vogue,* September 2007.

13. Ibid.

Lady O and King Bey

1. Evelyn Brooks Higginbotham, *Righteous Discontent: The Women's Movement in the*

Black Baptist Church 1880–1920 (Harvard University Press, 1994), p. 191.

Becoming the Wife

1. Anne E. Kornblut, "Michelle Obama's Career Timeout," *Washington Post,* May 11, 2007.
2. Jodi Kantor and Jeff Zeleny, "Michelle Obama Adds New Role to Balancing Act," *New York Times,* May 18, 2007.
3. Liza Mundy, "When Michelle Met Barack," *Washington Post,* October 5, 2008.

On Being Flawlessly Imperfect

1. Amy Cuddy, *Presence: Bringing Your Boldest Self to Your Biggest Challenges* (New York: Little, Brown and Company, 2015), p. 24.
2. Peter Slevin, *Michelle Obama: A Life* (New York: Knopf, 2015), p. 49.
3. Slevin, 325.
4. Slevin, 332.
5. Slevin, 312.
6. Slevin, 61.
7. Slevin, 236.
8. Slevin, 176.
9. https://www.youtube.com/watch?v=Hdl_W1BhpHw.

10. Slevin, 40.

11. Slevin, 182.

12. Slevin, 250.

Michelle Obama: Representational Justice

1. Michelle Obama, Remarks by the First Lady at Tuskegee University Commencement Address, Tuskegee University, Tuskegee, Alabama, May 9, 2015, https://www.whitehouse.gov/the-press-office/2015/05/09/ remarks-first-lady-tuskegee-university-commencement-address.

2. Anne E. Kornblut, "Michelle Obama's Career Timeout; For Now, Weight Shifts in Work-Family Tug of War," *Washington Post,* May 11, 2007, A, A01.

3. Susan Saulny, "Michelle Obama Thrives in Campaign Trenches," *New York Times,* February 14, 2008.

4. "Dismissing Her Critics, Mrs. Obama Forges Ahead," *New York,* February 23, 2013.

5. Michael Powell and Jodi Kantor, "After Attacks, Michelle Obama Looks for a New Introduction," *New York Times,* June 18, 2008.

6. Robin Givhan, "You Gotta Love the First Lady. No, Really, You Have No Choice," *Washington Post,* February 15, 2009.

7. Deborah Willis, "Michelle Obama in Photographs," in *Michelle Obama: The First Lady in Photographs* (New York and London: W.W. Norton & Company, 2010), pp. 15-17.

8. Jennifer Senior, "Regarding Michelle Obama," *New York,* March 23, 2009.

9. Winslow Homer quoted in Jean Gould, *Winslow Homer: A Portrait* (New York: Dodd, Mead & Co, 1962), 158. Also see Lloyd Goodrich, *Winslow Homer* (New York: Macmillan Co., 1944), 58.

10. Alain Locke, *The Negro in Art: A Pictorial Record of the Negro Artist and of the Negro Theme in Art* (1940; reprint, Chicago: Afro-Am Press, 1960, 1969), p. 205. Reviews of Homer's work from the nineteenth century predicted it. G. W. Sheldon concluded his 1878 account of the painter's work in *The Art Journal* that "his negro studies, recently brought from Virginia, are in several respects — in their total freedom from conventionalism and mannerism . . . — the most successful things of the kind that this country has yet produced." G. W. Sheldon, "American Painters-Winslow Homer and F.A. Bridgman," *The Art Journal,* vol. 49 (1878): 227. Also quoted in Mary Ann Calo, "Winslow Homer Visits to Virginia During Recon-

struction," *The American Art Journal* (Winter, 1980): 5. Two years later, *The New York Times* echoed the statement: "Mr. Homer shows his originality in nothing so much as his manner of painting negroes," *New York Times,* April 9, 1880, 5.

11. Sean Ross Meehan, *Mediating American Autobiography: Photography in Emerson, Thoreau, Douglass, and Whitman* (Columbia: University of Missouri Press, 2008), 133.